Heroically Well Adjusted
Confronting the Evolution of Insanity

Greg Langford

Editing and formatting by P.C. Zick

Cover design by Travis Miles, ProBook Covers

Contact: glangford60@yahoo.com

ISBN: 1523650273
ISBN-13: 978-1523650279

DEDICATION

To Amalia Alvarez, Ph.D.

I want to dedicate the ramblings you're about to read to Dr. Amalia Alvarez, the most interesting woman, scratch that, the most interesting PERSON I've ever met in my life. Maybe one day she'll tell her story, and you'll agree with that assessment. Without the experiences that Amalia has introduced me to and without her nonjudgmental open-mindedness when she hears my stories, I would have never considered putting all of this on paper. I could get into all the things we've done and places we've visited, but that's for her to tell.

Please write your book, baby. It'll be an inspiration for anyone who reads it.

Thank you, baby.

IN MEMORY OF

Amalie Alvarez Lehman

I also want to acknowledge Amalia's daughter, Amalie, a young woman who I never met, but whose death made it possible for Amalia and I to initially bond over the tragedies of suicide and mental illness, and then to grow to love one another.

May you rest in peace, Amalie.

TABLE OF CONTENTS

FOREWORD

My first cousin Judy Benowitz has retired and is starting her second career as a writer. She sent me a rough draft of her own story, *The Ties That Bind,* and her description of my family was such that I thought it perfect for the introduction to this book. When I read it, I cried uncontrollably to such a point that my fiancé thought I was laughing. I didn't wipe the tears. I'll let Judy start as a way of introducing my family.

The Ties that Bind

Excerpt from *Highway 11,* a memoir by Judy Benowitz

"Get outside!" The shouts from aunts and uncles would send the Langford cousins running, tossing, and tumbling through the house, rattling the walls from its rafters. Eddie, My surviving brother, Greg, Walter, and their big sister Deborah, by their numbers, would shake the foundation of Mama Harris' house.

My grandmother, Vida Melida Gertrude Perry Harris, who we called Mama, lived in a small wood-framed house that teetered on rock pilings two feet off the ground and was a wonderful place to explore for treasures underneath. Baby kittens were born there, and sometimes a snake lurked. The house had a back porch with a flat stone step in front where antique, pink, cascading petunias tangled. A wringer washing machine stood on that back porch for many years, and Mama would bathe us kids in a number two wash tub, when we spent the night. I stood up from my bath one hot summer night on that porch and Mama looked at my dirty face, "I have bathed all of you, even the crack of your ass, but I forgot your face." She laughed, and the sweet smell of her snuff-filled mouth, wide open, made me laugh too.

A large oak tree stood beside her house that was too tall to climb but provided a cool shady place to play, out of the hot Southern sky, until a swarm of wasps dropped like rocks from above and landed on your face with stinging, swelling pain that sent you running to Mama. She applied the medicinal Campho-Phenique cure, which smelled bad and did little to relieve the pain, but it was the smooth palm of that wrinkled hand that gently applied the oil that made you feel better even with a swollen face. All the cousins played outside when we visited Mama.

The Langford cousins were a formidable group when they traveled in a pack in their Daddy's Cadillac, the only car large enough to fit them all. They were maybe a year apart each and when they visited anyone's house, the boys ran fighting and tumbling with Deborah, the older sister, usually in pursuit.

Deborah was a smart ass who once called my Dad an "old fart." We were stunned by her lack of respect for her elders. Dad was angry at first, but he started thinking about what she said, and decided it might be true. He laughed. We all laughed. Deborah could be obnoxious—that's why I liked her so much. She was my first cousin and best friend, the daughter of Irene, who was my mother's—Ivah Ree—younger sister.

In the '60s, Deborah's parents, Howard and Irene, owned the Triangle Drive-In of Winder, Georgia; named such because it sat in the middle of a triangle of land between Highway 11 to Monroe and Highway 53 to Athens. Deborah and I spent a lot of time at the Triangle Drive-In. Irene made the best onion rings in the world. I watched her in the Triangle kitchen whipping up the creamy batter. The rings were cut large and wide by a machine, then she dropped them into the thick mixture, and they came out perfectly coated. She picked them up with a long stick through the hole of the rings, and they dripped until lightly coated in batter then into the hot oil. She watched them carefully picking up the basket to check their doneness. Crispy on the outside, the warm onion flavor took over your mouth.

All the Langford kids worked at the Triangle, as soon as they could reach the cash register. They were car hops on roller skates. Howard's mother, Mrs. Langford, owned the Winder Skate Rink next door to the Triangle, so all the kids were proficient skaters. In high school, the Skate Rink was home to the Friday night band "Bill Hartley and the Heartbeats." Every teenager from Winder and Monroe was there. The Triangle Drive-In was the destination for hamburgers. You could smell the burgers and fries for miles. Deborah's parents worked hard every day in the restaurant, and on the weekends they liked to go out to parties.

One Saturday night Irene and Howard were going out to for a formal evening. Deborah and I were supposed to babysit the boys. Irene looked beautiful with her hair up in a French Twist. She wore a low cut, blue brocade dress. She asked Deborah, "Does this dress make me look too sexy?"

"You're about as sexy as that telephone pole," Deborah said and stomped out of the room.

Deborah was often in charge of her four brothers, while Irene and Howard worked at the Triangle. Walter, at age two, grabbed the phone, when Irene called to check in one day. "Sissy won't change my diaper." Deborah laughed, as she and I took off running. I stayed many summer nights at Deborah's house, along with our cousin Ann, who lived down the road from me on Highway 11.

Ann's father, Perry Hugh, was brother to Irene and Ivah Ree. Ann and I took turns spending the night with Deborah who slept in curlers every night, and in the morning, she would tease and spray her hair into a stylish bouffant hairdo. She always had money for lipstick and perfume, very put together. With big brown eyes and dark brown hair she suntanned easily. She looked like Natalie Wood.

Deborah was a year younger than Ann and me, but she developed first with shapely hips and breasts. When we went with her to the pool, all the boys followed her. Ann and I were flat chested and slim hipped, late bloomers. There was always something to do at Deborah's house. She lived in the city of Winder and we could walk everywhere: to the record store, the pharmacy, and the movie theater.

The Langfords made lots of money from the Triangle Drive-In and the Skate Rink. Howard bought a new Cadillac every year to transport his large family. Irene bought expensive furniture. She gave Mother her old dining room set, when she bought a new one. Mother kept that furniture 'til she died. Before that we never had a dining room. We sat at the kitchen table that was pushed against a wall. At supper time, it was pulled out and five chairs sat around it. Four of them matched the table. The fifth chair was a ladder back cane bottom that sat lower than the rest. My brother, Wayne, occupied that chair. The Langford's dining room table rested on yellow carpet beneath a chandelier. Matching yellow drapes accented the window by the buffet.

Howard was a community leader and the owner of a thriving business. The Triangle sponsored one of the girl's-softball teams with Deborah as the catcher. Her uniform consisted of short-shorts and a blousy yellow jersey with TRIANGLE written on the back. Her catcher's mitt was as big as her head, and she could catch. I watched her play one night under the bright lights, and after the game a pretty blonde wearing lots of make-up came up to talk to us.

"Don't let my daddy see me talking to you. You have to leave." Deborah pushed her away. The girl was surprised, she thought they were friends. She walked away shaking her head. Howard could be strict with his rules, and Deborah found ways to get around them. She hung out with an older group of kids and was often in trouble with her dad.

Howard drove his family to Daytona Beach every summer. Ann and I took turns going with them. One hot summer Fourth of July, Howard and Irene drove their car to the dog races. Deborah and I were supposed to babysit the boys, but we took off walking the beach looking for our friends that we knew were in town too. Later that evening, we saw Howard's car driving on the sand back to the motel, and we started running to beat them home. We out ran the car and were in the motel when they came in. After everyone went to sleep, Deborah wanted to sneak out meet her friends.

"I don't think we should," I said, "we might get in trouble."

"Stop being such a baby. You're no fun. I'm leaving. Stay here by yourself." She climbed out the window. I hung my head out to see how she got down.

"Come on," she hissed. I smelled her breath. She smelled like milk and crackers.

I climbed out behind her. Since we were on the ground floor of the motel it was easy. We quietly tip toed past Howard and Irene's room and the boy's room which were dark. At two in the morning we walked down the wood ramp to the beach behind the motel. In the sand, still warm from the sun, I followed Deborah who walked fast and made a bee line to the Buccaneer motel. Deborah walked down the long side of the motel and tapped on the window of the lighted room.

"Hey, come on in," the pretty blonde from the softball game opened the window. We climbed into the small room with two double beds. There were four girls there. Deborah sat on the bed talking and laughing with her friends. I felt out of place since I didn't know these girls, and it was not unusual for Deborah to ditch me for her friends. I still liked being part of the escapade. We stayed out 'til four in the morning then climbed out the window and headed back to our motel. The stars were bright as we rolled through the window back into our room. Deborah taught me how to take chances and have fun.

Deborah was fifteen and learning to drive that year. She

wanted some time behind the wheel on our drive back from Daytona.

"I can just see the headlines now," Howard said. "Family driving to Florida dies in a car crash, being driven by the fifteen-year-old daughter."

In fact, Deborah did die in a car crash five years later while away at school. The family seemed to fall apart after that. Howard was never the same without his only daughter. Eddie, who stuttered as a child, was arrested for drugs. Another brother married at age sixteen. Greg stayed in high school and played football. Walter, the youngest kept to himself. I was living in Atlanta with my boyfriend, Bob, who, today, is my husband, when Mother called with the sad news of Deborah's death. Bob sat me down to tell me about Deborah. She was twenty-one and I was twenty-two. Deborah's funeral was my first experience with the death of a contemporary. I stood mute not looking at her in the coffin. I inched my way outside the church with Eddie, My surviving brother, Greg, and Walter trying to blend in. Greg explained to me that the boy in the car with Deborah died, too.

"Oh, really," I said.

"Yeah, really," he said angrily.

My voice was too casual. I tried to mask my feelings. Greg did no such thing. Deborah was like a sister to me. We were supposed to be in Ann's wedding that summer serving punch, instead my sister, Valerie, took her place.

In those years that followed, while I was away at school and living in Atlanta, Deborah's brothers drove the newest cars, when they turned sixteen. If they wrecked one, it was immediately replaced. Irene would complain to Mother in her affected southern accent.

"Eddie keeps wrecking his car. I got him another one, and he wrecked it too. He spent the night in jail for drugs."

I ran into Eddie in Piedmont Park, in Atlanta. In 1970, Piedmont Park was a hang-out for religious fanatics and hippies throwing Frisbees. My roommates and I had our Frisbees and hung out there too. It was also a place to do drug deals.

"Do you know Jesus?" a long hair asked.

"Yeah, I heard of him." I walked away not wanting to be saved. *What a creep.*

In a shaded area, under a big tree, I saw a skinny kid with long black hair and a pointed nose. He looked familiar.

"Eddie, is that you?"

"Yeah Judy, it's me," he laughed, "but you don't want to be seen with me."

His hair was very long, and I hadn't seen him since Deborah's funeral.

"What are you doing here?"

"I'm doing a deal. Get out of here. The cops are watching me."

"You have some pot?"

"Yes, Judy, I do. You need to go."

"Okay, but give me a joint."

"Jesus, Judy, here. Scram." He tossed a joint at my feet. I picked it up.

"Good luck, Eddie."

Eddie did time in the state penitentiary for dealing drugs.

He later married, and had a son. A successful business man for a time, he reminded me of Howard in the way he walked, talked, and conducted himself. While visiting me at Mother's house, when my dad died, he wore a suit and seemed very busy with his life. Five years later, he committed suicide. His son was a teenager. That next year, his wife's body was found in a burned car. She was not immediately identified. They were drug dealers. My mother related this story to me, when I came home for a visit. I was living in California at the time, away from the insanity that took over this family, after we grew up. When Eddie took his life, Mother was distraught, and my sister, Valerie called me.

"Do you think you can come home? Mother is going crazy. I need some help."

"I don't think I can get a flight out at the last minute. I'll come home in a few days after the funeral." The last thing I wanted to do was walk back into that nightmare.

Greg took Eddie's son to live with him. His son was the same age. Greg was married to his third wife at the time. The family closed the Triangle, and Daddy's Deli opened along with a laundromat, and a car wash. The three brothers worked those businesses together. Walter kept to himself.

"I can't deal with Walter anymore. He's on drugs and can't function. I have stopped answering his calls or seeing him," Irene complained to Mother.

Walter killed himself with a plastic bag in his mother's kitchen. When Irene found him she went into the hospital and never came out.

Mother related these stories to me over the phone. She wanted me to call Aunt Irene, whom I had not seen in years.

"Hey Judy." She sounded so small on the phone.

"How are you doing, Irene?"

"No good, I am no good."

"Do you remember when Deborah said you were as sexy as a telephone pole?" I asked trying to cheer her.

"Deborah was always saying something." She laughed weakly.

She died of a broken heart a few days later.

I had not seen Greg in years before Bob and I went to the Harris Homestead Heritage Day in Monroe, Georgia where I grew up. My mother's grandfather, John Harris, his wife, and six children lived in the farm house which dates back to 1823. Coker, my father's surname can also be found in the historic graveyard at the Homestead, but it is the Harris name that endures. The Coker name died with my brother, Wayne, who had no children.

Cousin Dotty restored the property and listed it on the National Registry of Historic Places. Events are held there such as: weddings and school field trips. Every four years, the Harris family reunion brings more than 200 Harris' to the grounds for a picnic and tour. When I saw the ad for the Heritage Day, I called all the cousins and asked them to meet me there. It was a good way to see everyone at once. Most of them still live on Highway 11, that swath of road between Monroe, and Winder, Georgia, where I grew up. You could follow the beer cans to Winder back then, because no liquor was sold in Monroe, but Winder had plenty of beer joints.

Greg and I have a lot in common. We are the only red heads in the Harris clan of cousins.

Greg's brothers, Eddie and Walter, committed suicide, and my sister, Valerie, did too-- though much later, only six years ago. We share a bond. I think we both try to understand our siblings, and how they ended their lives. Greg writes his stand- up comic routine for Atlanta night clubs. He told me he auditioned in LA for a comedy contest. He didn't win, but an agent approached him to play black night clubs in Atlanta. Greg's routine is based on suicide and addiction-- not exactly funny, but people can relate to it, so he has success. He told me about one time he pushed the envelope too far and insulted someone in the audience who called him out to fight. Greg left the show with a body guard.

Greg still looks fit, like an old football player. His hair has faded from red. The grey streaks make him a strawberry blond.

"I want you to come see my show, but the places I play are pretty rough."

"I've been to all black night clubs before," I said.

"I'm sure you have. I'll let you know when I play a nice club. Next weekend my show is in a place with valet parking just down from the Alliance in Atlanta. There's a strip club across the street. You might feel comfortable coming to that show," Greg said.

"We'll be in Boston next weekend, but I do want to see your act. Keep in touch," I said.

When Greg found out I was writing my memoir. He wanted to read my chapter on his family, so I sent it to him.

With love,
From Cousin Judy Benowitz

INTRODUCTION

To the reader—if there ever is one—you should know that I'm not sure if I'm writing this for your benefit or for mine. I've heard it said that a man needs a witness to his life. It's certainly been a truism for me. With all I've been through and continue to go through, I need someone to tell it to. I just need an audience to my life. I've attended numerous funerals, suffered through multiple divorces, and watched the natural order of life do its thing, so I'm running short on an audience. I thought it best to put this stuff on paper. I do know that I feel better just putting keyboard to screen—it used to be pen to paper, but like so much that I remember, things have changed.

Since I don't know who I'm addressing, I think I'll find it most comfortable if I use the vernacular that was used at the time of each story. I intend to tell this in the language used, which is that of a southern boy raised in a dysfunctional family in 1960s' Georgia. There's been a great debate on whether a man is more influenced by nature or nurture, but I'm pretty sure that vocabulary is a product of nurture. If you should continue to pay any attention to my ramblings, please be forewarned that you will be exposed to numerous instances for profanity. It's not my fault. I was raised in a home where everybody cussed. Hell, I can remember one time when my brothers and I were supposed to be getting ready for church, and my mother came in and yelled, "I'm tired of you sons of bitches." My reply was

"Damn, Mama, you shouldn't be so hard on yourself." I was probably nine years old.

I also remember being brought into the principal's office at school when I was in the second grade. They brought me and a couple of friends in and gave us a lesson on profanity. I remember telling the guy I didn't know what the hell the problem was.

So if profanity offends you, I will understand if you decide not to be a witness and quit reading now. This is not a politically correct manuscript either because it deals with suicide, addiction, and dysfunction. You'll be hard pressed to find me a politically correct suicidal, addicted, or dysfunctional person.

I'm hoping to accomplish a few things by putting my story on paper. My first hope is that I might find a peaceful place within my soul and finally become at peace with my past. My second hope is that others who have similar stories will find they aren't alone. Finally, I want everyone to see, including myself, that we have a weapon to fight these killers.

The reader should get a sense of my confrontational and sarcastic sense of humor. That's what I attribute my lasting so long in this world—my confrontational manner, my humor, and my work ethic. These traits have not only been my source of success, they've been my greatest curse. While they allow me to live, these qualities seem to alienate people. Being a hardworking, confrontational, smart ass has kept a lot of people at bay when it came to meeting the real Greg. Unfortunately, I've had to learn to laugh at the most inopportune times just to survive. Should the reader finish this and have an afterglow of pity, then I have failed my mission.

What I'm about to share is not a pissing contest, and in no way am I trying to make my challenges more dramatic or devastating as to whatever challenges that life has beaten you with. I hope we both share the philosophy of "it's not how we get knocked down in life that counts, but it's how we laugh at the ones or things that knocked us down as we're getting back up." It's that laughter that I hope to give to you the reader, to help you to begin your healing process with a smile. Once you can do that, you can begin to overcome your challenges. I hope you find weapons to protect yourself, defend your sanity, and help those you love from continuing to suffer the wrath of insanity.

Origin of Heroically Well Adjusted

I don't know if you ever saw the television program "Cheers," but it was a big hit in the 1980s. Cliff, the really weird and offbeat postman on the show, lived with his mother and was definitely a strange character. There was also a character on the show who you might remember by the name of Frasier Crane. Frasier was a psychiatrist, and later had the successful spinoff "Frasier."

During one episode of "Cheers," Frasier met Cliff's mother and was introduced to Cliff's family dynamic. After that experience, the psychiatrist looked at Cliff and said something to the effect of "after having met your family I've reassessed your situation and considering everything, I believe you to be heroically well adjusted." That hit home with me, and I thought it the perfect title for this book. Some of the things you're about to read may reflect negatively on me, and if I've told the story correctly, I should come off as a manipulative, self-centered, smart ass. I believe that after you meet my family, you'll agree it was those traits that allowed me to survive, and overall I'm heroically well adjusted as well, just as Frasier pointed out.

CHAPTER ONE - KILLERS IN OUR MIDST

I don't know how you would take it if you knew who the killers were that ended the lives of your mother, your two brothers, and your sister, but I'm pissed. These bastards have also killed my best friend and my cousin, and for the past fifty-seven years, they have been hiding in wait to kill my only surviving brother and me.

They almost got the surviving brother when he was twenty years old. I saved him at the last minute. They almost got me when I was forty. They put me in a hospital for twenty-seven days, and I've been in a self-imposed rehab ever since. It's gotten so bad that my only son has suggested it best that I not hang around his new family for fear these killers may endanger his wife and his two young sons. I'm almost agreeable to that proposition, if it will keep my son and future generations of my family from the cursed bastards that have ravaged the Langfords. Everybody that knows my family will tell you these two killers took their lives, but the bastards seem to stalk without fear of discovery. They are too strong for me to rid from this world, but I can at least get a little pay back if I can focus my anger and my skills to warn the world how do defend against these killers. I'm praying that my message will be taken as a survival guide and not the ramblings of a mad man.

The killers I'm talking about are mental illness, addiction, and suicide. Everyone knows who these killers are but are too ashamed or too blind to bring them into the public eye. There's a stigma associated with mental illness, addiction, and suicide. A stigma is defined as:

stig·ma ˈstɪɡmə/noun

noun: stigma; plural noun: stigmata; plural noun: stigmas

a mark of disgrace associated with a particular circumstance, quality, or person

So, mental illness, addiction, and suicide carry "a mark of disgrace associated with a particular circumstance, quality, or person," and we keep it quiet and secret to a point where we don't even acknowledge it when it's happening right before our eyes. Speaking of eyesight, an astigmatism of the eye can have the effect of causing vision to be blurred or distorted to some degree at all distances. That's a great way to sum up why people never testify against these killers. Their vision is blurred, and they are too disgraced to mention it to anyone.

If we agree that addiction, mental illness, and suicide carry a stigma, and we agree that the public has a certain blindness, or at least blurred vision on the subjects, then let's agree that these are uncomfortable subjects that few people openly discuss. It's like driving by a car wreck in reverse. In a car wreck, we don't want to see the scene, yet our eyes are drawn to the wreck, but when we approach the scene and the wreckage caused by addiction, mental illness, and suicide, it's just reversed. No matter how much we want to see the scene, our eyes automatically turn away because of the stigmatisms we carry.

I'm not going to let you get away with that when it comes to me and my experiences. It's never been my personality to be ignored. My confrontational attitude is that you may like me, you may hate me, but you aren't going to ignore me. I'm not just here to get attention for me, I'm here to bring attention to these killers. This is the story of my experiences of growing up with mental illness, addiction, and suicide, and I refuse to carry any stigma you might want to place on me. If you continue reading this, then I hope you're ready to have your stigmatism removed. I'm here to make you look at the crime scene, to see the carnage of despair, and the insanity of ignoring the circumstances that lead to the wreck. With any luck, just the fact that I would share so many personal stories might convince you to speak out and remove the stigma from yourself and your family.

You see, that's part of my strategy for fighting these killers. I plan to bring the insanities out into the public eye, and in doing so, help others to remove their burden of carrying the stigma. When we get others to share and acknowledge their struggles with these killers, then we move the topic into the mainstream, and out of the dark places where they are normally hidden.

I love card tricks, magic tricks, or just plain playing tricks on the world. I have a knack for finding the trick to just about anything. I also have an unhealthy sense of humor. Between the two of them, I've learned the trick of making a joke out of everything. My best friends, ex-wives, and everyone who has known me for a while will ask if I make a joke out of everything. They wonder how they can know when I'm telling the truth. My answer is that my jokes always center on the truth. My trick is making the harsh realities funny. I don't do it for laughs, I do it to survive. It's a natural reflex I apparently developed as a young child in order to endure. I'm a firm believer in Darwin and evolution, and I believe I evolved to be funny in order to fit my environment. Humor is my weapon against those two enemies. I'll tell the truth and make it a joke. If I can make people smile, I can help them think about these killers and hopefully help them begin their own personal recovery from their tragic circumstances. But first I have to find an audience and build my skill set in order to get their attention. So here's my resume for my quest.

Greg Langford's Resume

I've lived in seven decades.
My employment career spans fifty-one years.
I became an Eagle Scout back when it mattered.

I've not touched a sip of alcohol for the past seventeen years.

I've married and divorced three times.

I've outlived both my parents and three of my siblings.

I've buried numerous cousins, best friends, and lovers

I have personally been present at the unplugging of life support for my father, my mother, my oldest brother, my father-in-law, and my best friend.

I have a degree in economics from the University of Georgia, as well as diplomas from the Georgia School of Banking and UGA Banking School. I attended the Graduate School of Banking of the South at LSU.

I have a thirty-four-year banking career.

I've started and sold numerous companies, many for great gain.

I might have had success in business, but I've lost as much as I've made.

Here are a few more details to round out my life experience thus far: I was the first person baptized in the new baptism pool at Winder's First Christian Church in 1972. I earned the prestigious award of Eagle Scout in 1976 and became the captain of Georgia's track championship team in 1977. I graduated with a degree in economics from the most prestigious of universities of the south, the University of Georgia AKA UGA in 1981. My only son was born in 1985. I founded and became a chief lending officer of a bank in 1987. My first divorce came in 1989. I closed a savings and loan in 1991, and I earned four banking school diplomas by 1993. I started working with Atlanta's largest mortgage lender in 1994, and in 1995, I was their Rising Star for Sales. Life was good, but then came 'the crash,' beginning in July 1996 when my father died.

Twelve months later, my little brother, addicted to both drugs and alcohol, committed suicide. My mother died less than a month later of a broken heart. Then another year passed, and my oldest brother committed suicide in 1998, again because of an addiction to drugs and alcohol. I entered rehab in 1999. In 2000, I got divorced again. In 2001, my sister-in-law was murdered. In 2002, my best friend, Mike, and my cousin, Valerie, committed suicide—both victims of the enemy drugs and alcohol.

I forgot to mention something else, but this is probably a good time to bring up why only 'them Langford boys' were mentioned, and they didn't mention my sister. It's also why I was the first baptism at the church. My oldest sister Deborah was killed in a DUI-related car accident her sophomore year of college. I was only twelve years old then. That's the reason I was the first to be baptized in the church. You see, the baptismal pool where I was baptized was donated to the church in her name.

I'm in a unique position to speak on addiction, depression, and suicide.

I want to share that experience with you, but to do so, I need to go over my very interesting personal history.

CHAPTER TWO – THE EARLY YEARS
CHILD LABOR VERSUS CHILDHOOD

In 1964, I started school and began working at my father's establishment, the Triangle Drive-In Restaurant. For those of you who aren't familiar with the concept of a 1960's drive-in restaurant, let me describe the mood and the place to you. First of all, back in the 1960s in Winder, Georgia, there was nothing to do. No computers, only three television stations, and no cell phones. If you wanted to find people, you actually either had to go to their house or to the local hangouts. Since there were no shopping malls, the hangouts were much different back then. The car was everything back then as well, and the concept of pulling up to a restaurant, hitting a button, and having your food delivered by a 'curb hop' was hard to resist at the time. The concept of a hangout was irresistible for a teenager as well. My father put us all to work at the Triangle as either a cook, a curb hop, or helping out with cleaning and keeping the place running.

Back in the '60s of Winder, there were only two places to eat, the Triangle and the Dairy Queen. So every smart-assed high school kid with a car would cruise between the two. Picking on the little red-headed kid seemed to be part of the ritual. I was the red-headed kid, the only redhead of all of my parents' children, and that always distinguished me in the group. Needless to say, this dramatically affected my personality. There's a great story told by a friend who shares my birthday, but he is exactly six years older than I am. When he got his driver's license at sixteen, he took his first date to the Triangle. When they arrived, he noticed that the speakers weren't working so he asked this ten-year-old, red-headed kid if he was taking orders, to which I replied, "Hell no, I'm giving them." That story might give you some insight as to how I was raised.

There is absolutely no way you can understand me or my family without better describing the Triangle Drive-In Restaurant. It was the center of our life as much as our house and back yard. It was home. Every Langford child was born to work there, and the family dynamic centered on our 'shifts' at the Triangle. People from three counties have fond memories of the Triangle. I see folks all the time, even today, that tell me how they miss the food and the atmosphere. Their memories come from a different perspective than mine. When they were eating the food, it was my mother and the children who were working to cook it, when their food arrived it was my mother and the children who were working to deliver it, and when they left a mess, it was my mother and the children who were working to clean it. When they drove by and smelled the delicious aroma of fried onion rings, fried chicken, and various other delicacies, their senses danced. When you actually smell that way all day, it ain't so delicious. Work was the first trait of a Langford kid. I didn't walk home from the first grade, I walked to the Triangle. Seriously, if my father worked us like that now he'd be convicted of child labor laws in Singapore.

Daddy actually started the Triangle when he bought a little service station that sold beer and burgers as well. It was named the Triangle because it was surrounded by the state highway on one side, a little road that ran beside the railroad tracks, and a small connecting road. These two acres were shaped by the roads and made a triangle, thus the name. He put Mama to work cooking the burgers, and he managed the employees, the money, and the beer. At first, the place had a dining room and sold beer, but when the concept of a drive-in caught on, Daddy converted the place to a drive-in restaurant. At first, Daddy hired black cooks to help Mama and black boys from across the track to work as curb hops. Mama always had black maids help keep us kids so she could work at the Triangle. I'm not gonna get into any racial issues here, but I worked hard and was loved by black people through all of my youth.

Later, Daddy replaced the black guys with his children once we became old enough. Once Daddy started working the kids, Mama made him stop serving beer and get rid of the dining room. They wired the two acres with 'teletrays,' where you could mash a button from your car and order your food.

Inside, we had a switchboard where we could communicate with the customers to take their order, cook the food, wrap it, put it on a tray that hung onto a car window. Getting the order out meant that you then carried the food across two acres, delivered it, collected the money, and hopefully got a tip. Tips were instant gratification, and I loved and worked hard for them. I remember my first dollar tip like it was yesterday. I was maybe eight years old and was already working a lot at the Triangle. This big car pulled up with a couple and their four kids, and when I delivered the food, the father noticed I had on a very ratty pair of shoes. He gave me a dollar bill and told me to get a new pair of shoes. What he didn't know is that I had three pair at home and these were my 'scrub down' shoes. You see, every three months or so, Daddy would hold a scrub down of the place. This meant taking a hose from outside, putting Ajax and Clorox everywhere and scrubbing the place out. It was fun. The mixture of old grease and Ajax makes a great slippery slide. The intoxication from the mixture of chemicals made it even more fun, but it ruined your shoes. So I intentionally wore an old pair of my brother's shoes so as not to ruin mine. Once I got a dollar tip from wearing those worn out shoes, I wore them every day at the Triangle until I grew out of them.

Every year around July Fourth, Winder basically shut down. Not because of the holiday, but because all the textile mills closed for that week. Daddy always shut down the week of July Fourth, packed up the kids, a babysitter, and our pet Chihuahua into his Cadillac, and drove the eight hours to Daytona Beach. He'd go to the races, the dog track, and turn the kids loose with the babysitter. We all had a ball. All the kids had tip money, and each trip every kid had to buy the entire family a meal. Keep in mind a hamburger was twenty-five cents, so it really never cost more than five bucks or more. After school ended in late May, I'd work at the Triangle triple time and save my tips. It wasn't unusual at all for me to have fifty or sixty bucks in my pocket when I was eight and nine years old. I always had all this cash to blow in Daytona Beach, which I did gleefully. I remember one story of when I was around eight, and the family was eating at an ice cream shop. I stepped into the little souvenir shop next door and saw these white Gilligan-type hats. They were eighty-five cents each. I took five to the counter and asked the little lady how much. When she said "$4.42," I said, "No, ma'am, it's $4.38." She looked at me funny and asked how I figured that. I said five times eighty-five is four twenty-five, plus three percent sales tax of thirteen cents. So it was $4.38. She said, "Honey, sales tax in Florida is four percent, not three percent, but how on earth did you do that?"

I said, "Easy, it was five steak sandwiches."

It didn't get much better than that. It also didn't get much worse for me when it came to sunburn. Every year we went to Daytona, I got sun poisoning. My parents kept forgetting to keep the red-headed kid out of the sun, and the result was that they had to cover me in cold towels and call a doctor a couple of times. By the time I was nine, I was smart enough to figure out the problem. I have no idea why my parents couldn't figure it out the first eight years.

Daddy and Mama, with 'Them Langford Boys' – Middle step, from left, Eddie, me, and on top, Walter

I guess now's as good as time as ever to fill you in on the accomplishments of my three brothers and me. They used to say, "Them Langford boys, three of 'em are crazy as hell, and the other one is red-headed." I'm gray-headed now, but I used to be the red-headed one.

Langford Boy Statistics

Three out of four brother attempted suicide - Imagine a seventy-five percent suicide attempt rate.

Two of the four brothers succeeded in committing suicide - Imagine a fifty percent suicide success rate.

By the time the oldest one turned forty, they had accumulated:

- 24 DUIs
- 42 years of probation
- 14 totaled out vehicles
- 16 overdoses
- 14 trips to rehab
- 2 sentences to prison for over a year
- 39 shots fired
- 6 felonies
- 37 misdemeanors
- 75 malicious threats
- 1 trip to the Georgia State Mental Hospital in Milledgeville
- 1 city-wide power outage
- 1 brother who never attempted to take his own life (that's me)

The four boys also produced, sold, or consumed:

- 100 tons of onion rings
- 900,000 hamburgers
- 650,000 hot dogs
- 5 pounds of cocaine sold
- 7 pounds of MDA (the seventies' version of ecstasy)
- 1 / 2 ton of marijuana
- Laid down more ass than a toilet seat in the ladies room at Hartsfield International Airport

We had a sister as well, but Deborah Irene Langford died at the age of twenty in a DUI car accident while she was attending college. She only qualifies on the above list on the food part. She didn't qualify on any other lists, but I've got a suspicion it's only because she didn't live long enough.

Oh yeah, I guess I should mention that the four boys also produced:

- 1 Eagle Scout
- 1 captain of the state track championship team
- 4 high school track and field records
- 1 college track and field record holder
- 1 college graduate in economics
- 1 Habitat For Humanity's Man of the Year
- 1 fucked up former redhead. (that's me)

All of these are mine, except for one school record set by my only surviving brother.

Nature versus Nurture
or
It Takes a Village to Raise an Idiot

As a continuation to the debate as to whether personality is controlled by nature or nurture, I need to tell you the story of the history of the town where I grew up. After reading this, you may think that my family was doomed from the start by both influences.

Winder is a small town in northeast Georgia that was originally an Indian village that went by the name of Snoden. Once the white settlers found the place, they immediately kicked the Indians out, opened a bar, or a tavern as they called them back then. So Snoden became known as the Jug. After a few years, the settlers built a small inn to shelter all the drunks to crash for the night, and the town became known as Jug Tavern. It was called Jug Tavern for several years until there came an opportunity for the railroad to be routed through the town.

Once the local drunks at Jug Tavern heard about the railroad, they commenced to decide on how to outbid the nearest town in order to get the route. They approached the decision-maker for the railroad, and came up with a plan. Among other actions that we will never know about, the town council of Jug Tavern immediately changed the town's name to Winder. The railroad manager was delighted to run his tracks through the small town of Winder. Did I mention the last name of the railroad manager was Winder? It seems that the drunks had a plan up their sleeve and bribed Mr. Winder to get the track by renaming the town after him.

The generations of people who grew up and intermarried around the Jug, Jug Tavern, and Winder seemed to carry one genetic trait that carries to this day. A vast majority of the children of Winder have not only a genetic disposition to alcohol, but a cultural one as well.

There's a small headstone in the center of Winder showing where the county used to be part of three different counties until it was formed in the early 1900s. You see, the heart of Winder used to be located exactly on the line where three counties joined. Apparently back then, you could just take a step or two and you would go from Hall to Jackson to Walton counties. This created huge issues in regards to jurisdiction over the city. Apparently, the three other counties got together and decided they wanted nothing to do with those drunk bastards in Winder. They decided that each county would donate the land so that the drunks could form their own county and govern their selves. Imagine how bad things must have gotten if the three counties all decided to give up thousands of acres just to be rid of those drunken bastards from Winder.

I'm sure you've seen the National Geographic documentaries displaying cultural rites of passage. Some societies have adolescents climb a pole, tie their feet to a vine, and jump off. You're also familiar with the Jewish rite of passage of Bar Mitzvah. In Winder, the rite of passage for adolescents to enter adulthood is a competition to show your ass by getting drunk, stoned, or in some kind of trouble with the law.

That rite of passage often gave many of us either a DUI, a trip to rehab, or a little time behind bars. Like many cultures, this rite to passage often involves some sort of danger. Unfortunately, it's not unusual at all to hear that someone was locked up for a DUI, sent to rehab, died in a car wreck, or committed suicide, before they even make it to adult status. It's so common that we are rarely shocked to hear of such events.

Per capita to this day, Winder has more characters and four-way stop signs than anywhere in the world. I fit into that small group of people who survived the cultural influences of this small hamlet. It's true that I went to rehab, divorced three times, and have a DUI, but I've finally separated myself from this culture. With any luck and GOD willing, I will never again get another DUI, go to rehab, or die by suicide.

Another major goal I have is to validate my family's dysfunction, by making something good come from all of this terror, insanity, and death. The only thing I can come up with is to share with the world my truth and my philosophy about how to grow from being a victim of these killers to being a survivor.

The surprise in Winder is to hear that some kid grew up to be a successful, well-adjusted adult. I did find my way out, but only because I had adult influences outside of my family, and these mentors saved me from being another statistic. It was Boy Scouts and my scoutmaster that taught me that I could take my work ethic and succeed. It was sports that taught me that by setting goals, working toward them, and performing under pressure that I could be a winner. I've had friends tell me that I would have been a hell of a partier, if it weren't for sports. That's just ass backwards from what you normally hear.

If my message is delivered to the right audience, these stories can help others release their bondage, call out the kidnappers, and survive the horror of being held hostage by these killers. You can live without guilt if you work hard, practice tough love, and perform under the pressure of the addict's reaction to you as they realize that you are no longer supporting their insanity.

CHAPTER THREE – GROWING UP LANGFORD
(Apparently stupid is hereditary)

Ozzie and Harriet had their normal, and Howard and Irene had theirs.

Did you have a 'normal' childhood? Does anybody? Mine was normal for me, and yours was normal for you. What we saw on television, and what we've been told all our lives about normal families is a lie. The truth is that every family I know has had difficulties, and that's normal. I'm going to attempt to describe my family's normal. As you can imagine, having three suicide attempts out of five children, our normal was a little fucked up. This tragic climax of a family story didn't just happen on its own. There was a pre-amble to the story, and that's what I'm going to attempt to tell you.

I've researched, studied, and been told that the "normal alcoholic" family has children who take on distinct roles. That is the norm in an alcoholic family. One child takes on the caretaker role, another becomes the fixer, one will become the legitimizer and take on the role of being the good child in order to justify the family dynamic, and often there is a child who decides to be the rebel and act out negatively in order to get attention. My oldest sister Deborah became the caretaker. She bathed us, fed us, and while I never got but one spanking from my mother and none from my father,

Deborah whipped us. I became the fixer and legitimizer, and my brothers Eddie and Walter became the ones to act out negatively. They actually seemed to compete to see which one could be the worst. If Eddie got one DUI, Walter would get two. If Walter totaled a car, Eddie would total one, and when Walter committed suicide, it was just a matter of time until Eddie did the same. They had this sick ability to garner my parents' pity and their support. It's this blind support that Mama and Daddy gave each of their children that created the ability to continue their drinking, drugging, and insane behavior. If my parents had made their children realize that there were consequences to their actions, then we might all be alive today.

It might help you understand how insane it was to have grown up a Langford boy if I share a few stories about my childhood. Maybe a few war stories can better communicate how destined this family was to self-destruct and put too many of us in our graves.

The Story of the Pinto

I think this little story tells a lot about the thinking process of Langford men, and how all this insanity just may be hereditary. It's the story of my surviving brother's Ford Pinto.

During my sophomore year in high school, I had arranged to skip school with this cute girl. Other than agreeing to meet her before school that morning, I hadn't thought it out. I convinced my surviving brother to let me drop him off at his work, so I could borrow his 1975 Pinto. I had no plan, but at least I had a car. As the young girl and I were driving around that morning, she mentioned that her dad had a boat docked at a large lake about thirty miles away, so off we went.

I parked the car on a hill overlooking the lake, and she and I walked down in front of the car and headed toward the water when we heard the sound of tires rolling on gravel. We turned around to see the Pinto headed right toward us. She and I both ran to the front of the car and tried to stop its rolling down the hill when it turned to the right. I ran to the driver's side door and found it locked.

Grabbing the key out of my pocket and running at the same time now, I opened the door, and just as I did, the car rolled by a telephone pole. I jumped out of the way, and the door was slammed shut. The girl had jumped out of the way to keep from getting run over, and we both watched as the car rolled off a small cliff and plunged into the water. It was surreal watching the bubbles come up from the lake after the car disappeared.

I distinctly remember having to make the collect call to my parents that day. My mother answered the call, and when the operator asked if she would accept the charge from Greg Langford, she was apparently in shock. She kept telling the operator that Greg was in school. I finally yelled over the operator for Mama to take the call. I told her I had skipped school and wrecked the Pinto in the lake. She asked if everybody was all right and then handed the phone to Daddy. Daddy told me he would get a wrecker. I told him he'd need a scuba diver as well. It took him a couple of hours to get there, but when he did, he handed me the keys to his Cadillac and told me to get the girl back to school.

Daddy had to pick up my brother that night, and I remember as they drove up to the house and walked into the kitchen. I was following my surviving brother, trying to explain how sorry I was for having wrecked his car. He turned as if to hit me, but then started laughing at the top of his lungs. I had forgotten he had totaled our oldest brother's new Camaro when he had hooked out of school four years earlier. He thought it was funny that I had joined his infamous club.

When Daddy and I had a minute alone, he told me the story of how he had hooked out of school years before and had tied a mule to a wagon. The mule got out of hand, and the wagon damaged some man's car. He told me that it was just part of growing up. That would be a story in and of itself, but it goes on.

After we had the Pinto dried out, it drove just as well as before, although it did smell like fish for a while. About a year after my exploit, my oldest brother Eddie got a call one night and became very anxious to borrow my father's car since his was in the shop. Of course, Daddy wasn't stupid, and told him no. Eddie didn't give up and begged to borrow my surviving brother's Pinto. We didn't see Eddie again for two days, when Daddy got a call from the Georgia Bureau of Investigation.

It seems brother Eddie was in jail on conspiracy to sell more than two pounds of MDA, the seventies' equivalent to Ecstasy. But the story is about the Pinto. It seems that Eddie was promised $1,500 to drive a guy to the Waffle House in Lawrenceville. The story goes that the guy got out of the car, and when he entered the restaurant, he was surrounded by the Lawrenceville Police, the Gwinnett County Sheriff's Department, the GBI, and the DEA.

Apparently, at this point, Eddie decided it was a good idea to just drive off, and as he did, all hell broke loose. As Eddie told it, he cranked the Pinto, put it in gear, and slowly drove toward the exit when he heard a strange "clunk, clunk, clunk." It suddenly dawned on him that all these law enforcement officers had opened fire. Those clunks were the sound of bullets hitting the side of the car.

When the shots were finished, the Pinto had thirty-seven bullet holes including the ones in the block, radiator, two of the tires, several in the driver's side doors, and one through the head rest. Eddie was fine, but the Pinto never recovered.

The result was Eddie was finally convicted of a crime that daddy couldn't get him out of. The charges were too serious. Daddy eventually did pull enough strings to get Eddie incarcerated in a prison closer to Winder, and we were able to see him on occasion until he was released two and a half years later. When he came out, Eddie first tried to regain his old ways, and then finally chose his bottom. He straightened out, started a deli, got married, and had a kid. His new life started with a moment of clarity where he decided to take control of his life. It lasted about ten years before he once again slid in to his hidden world of addiction, which eventually led to his taking his own life.

CHAPTER FOUR – MY PARENTS

Howard Edward Langford SR. AKA Sly Howard AKA Daddy AKA the Colonel

November 13, 1927 – July 5, 1996

I think the best way to describe my father is to say he was one of the best men I ever knew when he was sober, and one of the sorriest sons-a-bitches walking when he was drunk. Howard Edward Langford, Sr. was the first born child of Carl B. and Carrie Langford. They were poor, mainly because of my grandfather's excessive drinking, which left Carrie to be the breadwinner of the family. Howard and his little brother Bobby grew up hustlers. If there were a dime to make in that little town of Winder, Howard and Bobby were there to squeeze it out. They would sell whatever they could get their hands on to make a profit: peanuts, men's suits, fireworks, food, and beer, you name it. Plus, they gambled a lot.

Daddy's favorite story about me was centered on the day I was born. He would gladly tell the story of the moment they handed me to him. They handed him this bright red-headed wrinkled little thing, and his first response was, "This ain't mine, y'all made a mistake." Like I said, I never fit in.

Daddy was a character in a town full of characters, and he took great pride in his little community and his ability to make a dollar. When he met Irene Harris (my mama—I'll tell you about her later), he found the perfect workhorse to provide him and his family with a decent living. He doted on her when he was sober, but when he got drunk, he would tell her, "Even a horse can work, but it takes brains to make a profit." And Daddy worked my mama like a horse. My mama worked like no woman I've ever seen. She always made a big deal that unlike all of her siblings, she never picked cotton, but she made it up by working unbearable hours at the Triangle. If you took the list of food that the Langford boys produced and multiplied it by ten, you'd only have about half of what my mama produced.

I'll share a lot of mama's story later, but right now I'm talking about Daddy. Howard had a strong public personality. He not only had a successful restaurant in town, he was elected to the city council and was mayor-elect several times over the course of his three decades of public service. He was actually elected twice after being busted in gambling raids at the local VFW.

Oh yeah, he looked just like Colonel Sanders as well. Everybody is famous in a small town, but Daddy really stood out. People admired his public service, his sense of humor, and his business savvy. He had a strong personality at home as well. We all looked up to Daddy, and he always provided for us very well. His protective nature and controlling personality are just two of the reasons us Langford boys could get away with so much. It never failed that once one of my brothers got into legal trouble, Howard would step into action. He either got us off or got the sentences reduced to a fine that he would pay. While I never used one of his 'get out of jail free cards,' the other brothers were never able to truly suffer the consequences of their actions. When Daddy died, they fell apart.

Daddy celebrating his resemblance to Colonel Sanders in the Winder Christmas parade

Regardless of this, I loved and admired my daddy. His favorite saying was, "There's two ways to go in this life, first class or half-assed, and it only takes a dollar more to go first class." My brothers proved that besides first class and half-assed, you could go through life dumb-assed. Daddy taught me to work, to dress well, and to never take abuse from anyone else. Right makes might as he would say. I can remember when the schools desegregated, he told me to "pick up a tornado if you need one, and don't take any shit off of anyone."

My favorite memories of Daddy are from when I was young.

The big deal when I was around five or six years old was when I got to go count money on Mondays with him and then have lunch. We'd drive down to the Triangle, and he'd bring out the money box from the weekend. I can remember the feel of the fresh air on the drive over, the aroma of a mixture of built-up grease and Ajax as we entered the building, and the excitement to be able to count the money. Daddy would hand me a stack of ones that smelled and felt like perfumed silk to me. I was so excited to be able to organize all of the bills, with George Washington facing up, counting the bills into stacks of fifty, and wrapping them with a rubber band. Daddy would recount the bills, and I can't remember ever missing on my count. By the time I was seven, I was counting fives, tens, and twenties with no problem.

Just like everyone else who had a father, I admired and emulated my daddy as much as I could. I remember just before Mother's Day when I was around six years old, he and I went shopping for Mama's present. We walked into a jewelry store and picked out a nice bracelet. When Daddy asked the owner how much it was, the owner said one hundred and twenty dollars. Daddy's reply was to ask how much if he paid cash. The owner lowered the price to one hundred and five. We then went to the local furniture store and found a nice lamp, and again Daddy asked the owner how much, and the owner said sixty dollars. Daddy asked how much if he paid cash, and the owner dropped the price to fifty. The next week, I was standing in line at the lunch room at school, and I asked the attendant how much my lunch was. She said it was fifteen cents. I asked her how much it would be if I paid cash. Needless to say, I didn't get a discount on my lunch, but I tried.

Daddy loved his children, especially Deborah. When she was killed in that car wreck, he was never the same. It always bothered me that while he still had four boys left, his focus was always on the loss of his only daughter. He was haunted for years after her death and couldn't sleep. He took to driving around nights and relied more heavily on the bottle than ever.

Looking back on it now, I'm amazed at how well Daddy always provided for his family. He kept us dressed well, put us all in cars, and we never failed to have a little spending money in our pocket. Daddy took us to Atlanta to eat, to watch the Braves play; and he often took us to the Fox Theatre. He even took me to visit the Governor's Mansion when Jimmy Carter was elected Governor. He sent me to Europe my senior year, and when I got my first banking job, he bought me ten suits, three pairs of shoes, belts, and ties to get me started. Howard was a good provider. But he was a dominant force with the children and allowed them to rely upon him too much. All of this would lead to ruin later in our lives.

After Deborah died, I took a more active role in the Triangle, which gave me a new 'shift' to work. I was now at the restaurant late nights, especially on weekends. While the day life as a Langford boy wasn't too bad, the nights were insane. Daddy apparently had only one rule when it came to alcohol, and that was never drink before dark, but after the sun went down, no rules applied. Working nights, I found out how insane alcohol drove everyone after dark.

Needless to say, I experienced a lot of unusual nights, but in particular there was one night that changed the dynamic of the family for me. It was a Saturday night when I was thirteen years old. I can remember that it was getting close to closing time, but we were still busy getting orders out. I had just came into the building from taking out an order. As I walked toward the cooler, I heard yelling coming from the stock room. I opened the stock room door only to see my father holding my mother in a head lock and hitting her in the head with a frozen pork chop. I didn't think to react as I bolted toward them and struck my daddy several times. I was crying profusely, and my entire body was shaking and tingling as I swung at him with abandon. When they separated us and the commotion calmed down, I realized that I had broken my father's glasses. They didn't tell me until years later that I also broke his ribs that night. I was never the same after that encounter, and for the rest of our relationship, I called Daddy by his first name of Howard. Somehow I realized that I could never talk to him while he was drunk, so I began lecturing him the morning after his bouts of drunkenness. I learned that he might listen while he was just realizing the damage he had caused the night before. I was hoping to shame him into that moment of clarity that I talk about now, only I was doing it at thirteen years old.

I guess I should tell you about how Daddy passed away. Apparently, all those years of smoking two packs of cigarettes a day while driving the kids around had caught up to him. Although he had quit smoking four years earlier, the doctors found a spot on his lung. He was too fat and out of shape for them to operate, and they gave him six months to live. They hit it pretty much on the spot because it was January when they diagnosed him, and he passed July 5, 1996. His health and strength had failed to a point that he couldn't take a bath. When my mother purchased one of those chairs that you put in the shower so that she could bath him, he made the comment, "Do you think I'm going to put up with this shit?" In other words, life for him was no longer worth living, and he gave up his will to live. That was just two days before the ambulance came to the house to pick him up.

He had lost his will to live, and within a week, he had fallen into a coma, a coma, which my mother blamed on me. Here's how that went down. I took my father-in-law, who was dying of cancer, to visit my parents up at their retirement home in the mountains. We had driven up on July 3 and planned to return home that evening. That didn't happen. As we arrived, my father was feeling especially weak, and I went into the bedroom to visit. We spoke for a minute or two while he was sitting on the side of the bed, and then he called my mother into the room. As they sat there with his arm around her, they talked of how much they'd been through and how much they loved each other. My father then told my mother to call the ambulance.

I'll never forget following the ambulance to the hospital. My father-in-law was riding with me as the ambulance proceeded down the highway. Suddenly the lights on the ambulance started flashing, and the ambulance started hauling ass. I pressed hard on the accelerator just to keep up with them.

As we wheeled into the entrance to the emergency room, the ambulance that was just in front of me opened its doors. Two attendees were waiting there, and as they opened the doors, they pulled my father out of the ambulance and immediately started doing mouth-to-mouth and chest pumps on him. They rolled him into the hospital, and we followed, with me in shock.

Once we were in the hospital, a doctor approached me and asked if my father had a living will. I didn't know if he did or not and really didn't know what he was talking about. He explained that it was up to me to decide to keep him alive or unplug the life support. I immediately told the man to keep him on life support. I then broke down and don't remember much other than a nurse giving me a sedative, and my mother and little brother arriving a little later.

When I met them in the parking lot, my mother was distraught. I had called the house earlier and let Walter know what had happened, including the part about the life support, and my decision to keep Daddy alive. You could tell that Mama was more mad than sad. As I approached her with probably the saddest expression on my face that I had ever had, she lit into me like you wouldn't believe. Her exact words were, "What the hell were you thinking keeping your daddy alive? He had a living will so he wouldn't have to suffer."

My sadness turned to a combination of fear and anger as I realized what she was telling me. I felt all the guilt, anxiety, and insanity wash over my entire being. I don't know if I can describe this emotional state that I go to when this insanity overwhelms me. I've experienced it over and over since I was a child in this family, so I may have enough experience to explain it. It's like this hazy layer of invisible gook is attached to my skin. I can feel it when I move, it's like a cloud attaching itself to my body. My mind goes into an adrenaline induced state of activity, and I can't attach myself to any thought other than survival and retreat. I either react with rage or complete withdrawal—there is no in between. I was supposed to let my father die—a decision I couldn't make on my own had just become a decision I had made by mistake. By not letting them unplug Daddy, I had made the decision that would keep him alive in a coma for another two days. Mama had the doctors unplug the life support, and we sat there for two days watching his lifeless body heave up and down as he struggled to breath. He passed away during the night with everyone asleep. I didn't come out of my fog until well after the funeral. When I did, I was left with only despair and a plan. A written plan.

My Memoriam to Howard, my Daddy

When my father died in July 1996, it greatly affected me, and I wanted to lash out. As we were leaving the funeral, I told my wife at the time that Daddy had been a character. He looked just like Colonel Sanders, and Daddy had loved the city of Winder, serving as councilman and mayor-elect for more than three decades. I wanted to do something to remember him by. I asked her not to think I'd lost my mind if the situation ever came up for me to act like a character and represent the city of Winder. I warned her that I was going to go out of my way to create a commotion. From there I went into the house, opened a bottle of Crown Royal, and commenced to get drunk.

Believe it or not, about three months later the opportunity presented itself when an article came out in the *Atlanta Journal-Constitution* that was less than flattering to the city of Winder. The article was about the sophisticated side of Winder, or lack thereof. It seems that the president of Blockbuster Video had an article in *Fortune Magazine* where he stated that Blockbuster was going to differentiate their product mix based on the market area of the store. His exact quote was, "We will have a more sophisticated product mix in New York than say Winder, Georgia." Well, this was exactly what I needed to act a fool, represent Winder, and honor my father. The way I saw it, I had permission from the dead to act a fool, and I took full advantage of it.

My first move was to start a foundation called, The Society for the Advancement of Values that Winder Affords, or SAVWA, and I organized a fair—a SAVWA fair. I went to the city of Winder and got a permit to demonstrate on my own land directly across the street from the Blockbuster store. I organized a boycott of the store, and, since it's the new south, I had a 'girlcott' as well. You can imagine how excited I was when I actually went to the sporting goods store and found a blue and a pink cot for sale.

My plan was to invite the president of Blockbuster to Winder. My thought was that since he's never been here, then he should drop by and judge our level of sophistication for himself. So I put together a plan for an all-expenses paid—once he got there—vacation to Winder. I decided to have 'dinner on the grounds' on a Sunday, and I invited Bill Fields, the president of Blockbuster.

Once I got the permit and set the date, I went about getting sponsors. I got Bee Bum, the local funeral director, to donate a tent and a Hearse Limousine for Mr. Fields. I got Greg Willoughby at Ol' Wills Bar-B-Que to donate barbeque, stew, and slaw. I got Polly Jones at Bob's Tire to donate a set of re-treads in case he decided he wanted to 're-tire' here, and I got Claude Tuck, the owner of a local haberdashery to donate a pair of size fifty-eight bib overalls for Mr. Fields. Claude told me that if they weren't big enough for his big city ego, he would get us a bigger size.

I made a video tape—VCRs were the rage back then—and sent it to Blockbuster's Corporate Headquarters in Ft. Lauderdale, Florida. I contacted the local papers, the writer of the article in the *Atlanta Journal-Constitution*, the editor of *Fortune Magazine*, and the Atlanta radio stations. In addition, I petitioned the Winder City Council to present the 'Key to the City' to Mr. Fields, if he came for a visit. The City Council turned me down, so I got Eric Patrick, the owner of Patrick's Gulf Service Station to loan me the key to the men's room to present to Mr. Fields.

So when the day came, I had the tent, the food, a bunch of tires, a limousine, the blue and pink cots, and a demonstration of our culture through exhibits, such as cultured buttermilk in champagne glasses and a 'poultry reading.' I had heard that these big city folks considered it high class to go to poetry readings. Since most poetry I knew had been written on bathroom walls, I decided to do the next best thing. I had a 'poultry reading.' This area of north Georgia is the poultry capital of the world. We produce more chickens than anyone else does, so I set up a chicken in a cage lined with the *Atlanta Journal-Constitution* and set up a *Fortune Magazine* for him to read. As many chicken farms as we have around here, I had hard time finding a small chicken to put in the cage. I ended up borrowing one from a local reptile house. The chicken was on reprieve from being eaten by a small python.

At the end of the day, there was no Mr. Fields, only eight of my closest friends dropped by, and I had two cars stop thinking it was a flea market. The only bright side is that I sold the tires for ten dollars. I left a little disappointed, but at least I showed the chicken a good time.

I was going to drop it there, and call it a day. I made my point, but apparently the spirits of my father decided I wasn't through because the very next day, I got another message from my daddy. I went in for a haircut, and my hair dresser had a present for me. It was a copy of the *Palm Beach Post* with a headline of "Even Hicks in the Sticks need a Blockbuster now and again." It was the exact same unflattering article that the *Atlanta Journal-Constitution* had posted, but the headline had been changed.

I re-gathered my focus and contacted the Ft. Lauderdale city manager's office and got a permit to demonstrate, boycott/girlcott Blockbuster at their corporate headquarters. In addition, I contacted the editor of the *Palm Beach Post* and gave her a piece of my mind. The bottom line I had with her was that she might think I'm a hick from the sticks, but I proved I could be a prick.

My next move was to set upon the media in Atlanta. I started calling the morning radio talk shows on my way to work each morning. I ended up on Star 94, Z 93, Q105, and 97.1 FM's morning shows, in addition to three of the local talk shows. I would call and get into any contest they were having and then hi-jack the show and start bitchin' about Blockbuster. By the second call, every station would keep me off the air, except Star 94. For some reason, the disc jockey took a liking to me, and I became a regular caller. He even started introducing me as the Mayor of Winder.

After a little media coverage, the vice president of Public Relations at Blockbuster finally contacted me. I don't remember the guy's name, but man, I mean, he was a slick character. I wrote Mr. Fields a letter telling him that if we could mass produce that guy we could put Teflon out of business, he was that slick. In any event, this guy tells me that if I come to Ft. Lauderdale that I won't be welcome. I made it a point to tell the guy that all I was doing was inviting Mr. Fields to visit Winder, and that it was un-neighborly of him to not show the same consideration to me.

What I found out was that Mr. Fields was currently working on relocating Blockbuster's corporate headquarters away from Ft. Lauderdale and was drawing a lot of flak from the local media, their employees, and their customers. I guess having me and my chicken down there would only add to their problems. So I scheduled the date, booked the flight, hotel, and car, and let the slick guy know we were coming down.

Just a few days later, and about a week before our trip, I get another call from Blockbuster's PR man. He tells me that Blockbuster wants to schedule a Winder Appreciation Day on the same date I'd scheduled my protest in Ft. Lauderdale and wants to know if I'll attend. I asked him if Bill Fields would be there, and he tells me no. My response was that I'd have to contact my media advisor and get back to him. After we hung up, I called my twelve-year-old son and told him about the offer. His first question was, "Is that man coming?" When I said no, his response was "Well, that ain't right," and that was all I needed to know.

I contacted the PR guy and let him know that I wouldn't attend the Winder event unless Mr. Fields was there, and that I was continuing with my plans to demonstrate at their corporate headquarters in Ft. Lauderdale. An hour later, he called back to let me know that Mr. Fields had changed his mind and would attend the Winder event after all. Once I had him confirm it to me and the press, I told him it was too late to cancel my trip. I then asked him if he could give Mama, my boy, and me a ride back on his private jet. Needless to say, they declined my offer, so Mama, my son, and I flew down to Miami.

The afternoon I was to meet Mr. Fields, I could distinctly see my daddy laughing his ass off and smiling proudly for me as I finished pumping the gas and headed to the house to get ready for Mr. Fields to meet me. I had rented a limo, put on my tux, bought a twelve pack of Michelob, picked up my son and his cousin, and headed to the local Blockbuster. The place was crowded when we arrived. Once we pulled the limo to the front entrance, several reporters came out to greet us. I made it a point to stay within the darkened limo for several minutes, while I polished off a couple of beers before we exited and went into the store. As the photographers flashed pictures, several guys in suits surrounded Mr. Fields and myself while the reporters asked a few questions. I was given about one hundred free video rentals and the largest Blockbuster Membership Card I'd ever seen.

That night I returned to an empty house, sat out on the back porch while the torch lights swirled from the Blockbuster Store's Celebration. I was all by myself, but I could feel my daddy looking down on me and smiling. The next morning, I walked out to get the morning paper and my picture with Mr. Fields had made the front page of the *Atlanta Journal-Constitution*. I had knocked India and Cuba off the front page. I learned later that day that three other local papers had covered the event on their front pages, too. Later that week, I found out that *The Palm Beach Post* had covered the story as well. I guess I wasn't such a prick after all.

If you've ever been around a manic person, you may have noticed that they seem to act as if the only thing that matters is the thing that they are focused on achieving. That was definitely true of me in the way I threw myself into getting Mr. Fields to visit Winder. My focus for almost three months was on getting the result I wanted. Like most episodes of my manic binges, I would sometimes along the way have a moment where I realized how insane I was acting. I can only say that it was and continues to be difficult for me to act in an insane manner, but yet be smart enough to know that I'm acting insane. Being smart is one thing, being insane is another, but being smart enough to know you're insane, is a hugely defeated place to be. Each time I realize I'm behaving insanely, it's like waking from a dream state. I'll look back on my actions, measure the damage, and make a decision to continue or to let it go. Unfortunately, letting go is not my strong point. All too often when I do 'snap' out of it, I find myself too far into the project to quit. It's a reoccurring theme with me.

Dorothy Irene Langford AKA Mama AKA Miss Irene

November 14, 1930 - August 9, 1997

Daddy was raised in a home with a drunken father and a mother who had to be the breadwinner, and to a large extent, he created the same scenario when he married my mother. While Daddy was a better business man than his father, he still relied on Mama as the work horse that all of his success was based upon.

Dorothy Irene Langford was born on the poor side—and by that I mean dirt poor—of the Harris family who first came to Georgia in the late 1700s when our great, great, great, great grandfather came here on a land grant given to him for serving in the Continental Army. Her father was dirt poor and liked to drink hard. I guess she was looking for what she knew when she married my father.

The earliest story my mother ever told me about myself was of how I reacted as just an infant to her leaving me in the car while she worked at the Triangle. Apparently a couple of weeks after having me, she went back to work and took me along with her. She would tell the story of how quiet and peaceful I was while she worked and toiled in the kitchen. The way I figure it, I was probably just happy to be in a quiet place after being toted around in her belly for the previous nine months. It couldn't have been quiet in there.

I also know that Mama came from a large family of seven children, all of whom were born dirt poor. Besides the stories I heard about my grandfather, Walter Harris, who died before I was born and was an obvious alcoholic, I'm pretty sure that her four brothers were alcoholic as well. Whether they died from cirrhosis of the liver, drowning, or falling off the back of a pickup, it was liquor that got 'em. One brother drowned while fishing in a boat, and the other fell out of the back of a pickup truck while returning from a fishing trip. I can only guess that it was either the fishing or the drinking that killed them, and neither of them had swallowed any worms unless there was some tequila there. Anybody see a resemblance between the four Harris boys and the four Langford boys? I think I see a pattern.

I can tell you stories of the insanity that she put up with, and I probably will, but I want to share one story that tells of her shame, and how she handled it. It has to do with my failing the first grade and the circumstances surrounding that event.

It had always been a source of embarrassment for me that I failed the first grade. That failure played a big part in my life for a long, long time. To be honest, it still is the reason I resent a lot of things. It instilled in me a sense of shame and a feeling of 'less than' with the class that went on without me. It also placed in my personality the need to prove that I am just as good as anyone else is, even though my family told me that I wasn't.

When I was thirty-five, I was sitting with my mother and asked her how it was that I could be so smart, graduate with an economics degree, hold four banking degrees, and have a successful career, and then fail the first grade. She looked at me with a firm expression on her face and said, "You didn't' fail. I held you back." When I asked her why, she began telling me the story of my first day at school. She said my homeroom was filled with the mothers of kids whose fathers included two doctors, a pharmacist, three lawyers, and a couple of kids whose fathers owned or managed the large textile plants in town. She started telling me how well they were dressed, and how they all seemed to know each other. She told me how ashamed she was to be a working mom when all these women were well off. Her exact statement to me that night was, "I knew right then I wasn't' going to put up with those bitches for twelve years, so I held you back." I guess it never occurred to her to tell me that I didn't fail, and she passed her shame to me.

That explained a lot to me as to why I always felt so driven and held such a strong resentment toward people born with a 'silver spoon' in their mouth. While it might have explained the why about my personality, it came a little too late to change the man. I still have a feeling of 'less than' in almost every social situation that I encounter. It's a fact that I walk with a chip on my shoulder, and it seems that I'm always ready to 'prove something' everywhere I go. My brothers and I were always instilled with a work ethic and resentment that we weren't as good as everybody else was. Mama was ashamed that we had to work, and she passed that on to us, but Daddy always taught us to stand up and not take any shit off of anyone. Between the two parents, us Langford boys were prideful in our inferiority. We wore it like a fire alarm button. Just push it once, and all of our insecurities went into action. When that happens, insanity rules the day.

I had no idea what my mother went through until shortly after Deborah's death. It was then that I saw how hard my father worked her, how abused she was, and how my brothers all took her for granted. It affected me in more than a few different ways.

Let me give you an example of my family's interaction and an insight into the addicted mind. When I was in college, working four nights a week at the Triangle, living in a mobile home with my first wife, I was paying someone to cut my grass. I drove to my parent's home, and even though Daddy and my three brothers were living there, I found my mother cutting the knee-high grass. It wasn't enough that she worked eighty hours a week, fed them, washed their clothes, and cleaned up after them, she had to cut the grass as well. I couldn't believe how none of them seemed to care about how the house looked or how unfair it was for Mama to have to cut the grass. I stopped my mother, and I began cutting their grass on a regular basis. Remember I'm the fixer, and high grass doesn't give a good public perception, so it was right up my alley. But here's the screwed up part, each brother came to resent that I was cutting my mother's grass. They raised so much hell that Mama ended up blaming me for causing the ruckus and told me to please not help out. I couldn't win with this family, but at least Daddy ended up hiring someone to cut their grass so Mama wouldn't have to cut the yard herself.

I remember finding Mama sleeping in the laundry room because Daddy had come home drunk and abusive. I have to admit though, that she held her own as well. She would pack her twelve- and nine-year-old boys into the car at midnight just to drive to the local VFW to, as she put it "go get your damn daddy." Apparently, some of my dad's friends would call her when Daddy got too far out of line, in either his drinking or his gambling.

I can remember one night while working at the Triangle when my mother and my daddy's mother got into a big fight. They were cussing, yelling, and throwing brooms. As I was taking an order to a customer, he casually asked if there were witches fighting inside. Another memory is of one morning we found a couple of bullet holes in Mama and Daddy's bedroom wall. Apparently, Mama had found the gun in the middle of a fight, and fired off a couple of shots. That's my mom!

I guess I should tell you the story of Mama's death. It began with little brother Walter's suicide in her home. When Mama called to tell me about Walter dying, I dropped everything and drove to her mountain home. She and Daddy closed the Triangle, sold their house in Winder and moved to the mountain community of Blairsville,

Georgia, just a few years earlier. It shocked everyone when they moved, but Daddy was determined to retire in solitude. Mama rejected the idea from the start. The funny thing is that just after a couple of months, Daddy began getting restless and wanted to move back to Winder, but Mama would have none of it. She had found new friends, started preserving vegetables, and making homemade jellies. She was in heaven up there, and she refused to move back home.

When I got there, she was already packed, and there was no crying going on. She was full of anger and despair, but not emotionally distraught. We gathered things and headed to my aunt's house where she would stay and organize the funeral. At least that was the plan.

What actually happened is that within an hour of our being at my aunt's home, Mama had a "spell." She fainted, and we rushed her to the hospital. The doctors thought she was having a stroke and rushed her to Athens Regional Hospital where they could treat her better. It was the hospital where my brothers and I met for the first time since Walter had died. It was not a great reunion.

I was sitting in the intensive care waiting room having followed the ambulance to the hospital when my brothers walked in the room. There might have been other people there, but that didn't matter. They walked in together, and apparently they had decided that it was my fault that Walter had killed himself and Mama was here. It was like cutting the grass all over again. My surviving brother wanted to fight, and Eddie was so fucked up on his pills that he could barely talk. Neither asked about Mama. They just directed their anger at me. I was defiant, hurt, and scared. I left the room and checked on Mama. When all our wives arrived later, things calmed down, and I returned with them all to the waiting room.

We set up a schedule for who stayed and who went home. I stayed at the hospital without leaving until late the next day when they had Mama stabilized and told us that there was no stroke. Eddie and my surviving brother had arranged Walter's funeral for the next day. I was completely exhausted, and at the same time, in such a manic state that I didn't know whether to rest or go on a binge to fix all this. When I arrived home, my house was full of people. You see, my wife and I were mortgage bankers, paid solely on commission. She was having her biggest month ever, and these people were in our home office. She was too busy to comfort me.

The next day was Walter's funeral. Although they had moved Mama into a private room, she couldn't make the funeral. The funeral parlor was full, but to tell you the truth, I've noticed that I don't remember the actual funerals too well. They all seem surreal to me, like a dream I can't recall but keep getting little remembrances of.

My second wife and I had people come to our house after the funeral. Since ours was the only house large enough to hold a crowd, the wives all decided that it would be best held there. A lot of Walter's old friends dropped by, all of my buddies were there, and it was a nice remembrance of Walter. He had a lot of drinking buddies, and they all had a lot of stories of the crazy stuff he had done. As sad as the end result might be, the antics of an alcoholic can be funny as hell. Eddie never made it because he had passed out in the car after the gravesite services.

When everyone left the house, I headed to the hospital to visit Mama.

I'll never forget opening the door and entering Mama's hospital room. She was wearing one of her long silk nightgowns with floral prints, watching the television when I entered. I came in and her first words were "Damn, you didn't bring me any leftovers." I couldn't help but laugh out loud. We visited for a while and talked about a lot of things that I don't remember now. I do remember telling her that I was going to leave for a couple of days and get my thoughts together. She was in good shape and was to be released in two more days anyway. I had no quiet place to go because my home was no longer a haven, so my wife had called several friends out of state to see if I could visit. One buddy in Orlando invited me down. I was on a plane the next morning.

I spent three days trying to get my act together. Everyone and everything seemed to aggravate me, and I was a mess. It took two days for me to organize my thoughts, and on the third day, I had a written plan, and I jumped back on the plane. I had not spoken with anyone other than my wife for three days. But she only returned my calls between clients and calls from my friends and family.

My leaving might have been cowardly, but it did rebuild my confidence that I could handle all the pressures I was feeling. I made my plan the second day in my buddy's apartment while he was a work. Sitting there all by myself and in a quiet place, I was able to write down each issue that was eating at me. I was sweating my income and wrote down all my holdings. I could last a year. I was worried about Mama being in the mountains all alone, and I wrote a plan to get her into an assisted living center closer to me. I wrote a plan for dealing with my surviving brother's anger toward me. The one that really had me in a quandary was Eddie. I wrote down that I'd possibly get him to rehab, and ask if he would give me guardianship of his son. I combined all my notes, put them on a small paper that would fit into my wallet, and returned home a little more composed and confident.

Once I landed in Atlanta, I called my wife who told me that Mama had pneumonia and had slipped into a coma. I drove the ninety miles to the hospital flashing my headlights and driving as fast as I could. As I came into the waiting room, my surviving brother jumped up and yelled, "Where the hell have you been?" He started towards me as his wife pulled him back. My plan for him wasn't going to work right now.

Apparently, Mama's pneumonia had been resolved, and the fluid had been mostly removed from her lungs, but now she had gone into renal shock. From what the doctors told us, she had something wrong internally, and they had to operate. He was going to operate to save her. It suddenly occurred to me that my last conversation with her was the day of Walter's funeral, and that I had abandoned her. I might not have wanted to, but I had become another victim and survivor of Walter's suicide.

They took Mama to surgery immediately, and my surviving brother, Eddie, our wives, and I wandered like zombies between the smoking area and the surgery wing. We were too distraught to argue. For once, we were on the same page. After about two hours and several packs of cigarettes smoked between the three of us, the nurse finally came out and told us that Mama had been taken back to the intensive care unit, and the surgeon would meet us in the waiting room there.

After just a few minutes, the surgeon joined us with a very determined and grim expression on his face. He told us that septic shock had set in and that Mama would expire without another surgery, but that even with another surgery, she would have less than a fifty percent chance of survival. As he was leaving us to discuss our options, I asked if we could see her. He agreed, and we all went to see Mama in her room. All six of us gathered around my mother's bed and tried to talk with her, but there was absolutely no response. She was comatose. The doctor asked if we wanted to consider taking her off life support. I agreed and made the statement that she had gone through enough. Mama actually made a grunt and a small nod of her head. She was telling us she had had enough and to let her go.

Somebody asked the nurse if the doctor was still on the floor, and she went to retrieve him. We told him our decision, and to our surprise, they were prepared to disconnect her from life support and did it while we stood there. It was the saddest moment of my life. We all stood there crying and holding hands as you could see Mama's breathing slow and hear the beat from the heart monitor decreasing. The beats slowly wound down to a point where she went flat line and passed with no physical reactions. It was as if she had just fallen asleep to escape the nightmares of her life and join Howard, Walter, and Deborah in another dream.

It took the doctors at the hospital more than four weeks to produce a cause of death. I kept telling them to just write down broken heart and loss of will to live. Apparently, they didn't have that one on the list of causes. The truth is Mama had it in her mind to die, and her mind was committed to killing her body. First, the mind forced her blood pressure up, but the doctors had controlled that. The mind then told her lungs to fill with fluid, and again the doctors were there to control that. Finally, the mind pulled out all stops and shut down her other organs. Her loss of will to live, her mindset, and her grief over Walter had killed her. That would have been the proper diagnosis for her cause of death.

CHAPTER FIVE – MY SIBLINGS

Deborah Irene Langford

July 23, 1950 - November 11, 1970

Deborah Irene Langford was the first of five children born to
Howard and Irene Langford, and the only daughter. Being the first
born and the only girl brought along special privileges,
responsibilities, and demands for this bright and cheerful girl. She
was tragically killed in a car accident when I was twelve, so I can't
speak too much about her short life, only to say that she helped raise
me. I both adored her and feared her, and I never told her good-bye
when she left that fateful last time to head to college. I can speak
volumes as to how her death affected our family, and to how none of
us would ever be the same after she was gone.

What little I do remember of Deborah is that she was Mama
and Daddy's pride and joy, as well as a surrogate mother to the four
little brothers who were to come along. Deborah changed our
diapers, cooked our breakfast, and whipped our asses. She was like a
mother to me, and she seemed to take pride in doling out her
punishments. I loved her, depended on her, wanted attention from
her, and feared her. I know she was bright because she was going to
college, I know she was funny because her high school class voted
her wittiest, and I know she was a hard worker, because that's just the

way Howard and Irene raised their kids. What I didn't know was that she was a witness to the alcohol abuse by my parents and their constant drunken brawls. Mama told me later that Deborah had always tried to get Mama to leave Daddy. I also didn't know that after her death, I would inherit her role of both family jester and family justifier. Someone in the family had to be the one to present to the community as a success, with Eddie and my older brother acting out in all of their 1970's glory of sex, drugs, and rock and roll,. the role of representing the family dynamic was doled out to me at the ripe old age of twelve. Deborah had had that role, but she had died. The Queen had died, so long live the King. I became a Boy Scout, a track star, and college-bound at eighteen, all as I worked basically full time at the Triangle.

Perhaps my strongest memory of Deborah is of the last weekend she was home from college and was leaving to go back. I remember playing in the yard, her standing by her packed car, and asking me to hug her good-bye. Just as any little red-headed brat of twelve would do, I refused to give her a hug, and she drove away. It's weird that just after her car left my view of sight, I got this strange feeling that I needed to tell her bye. I ran inside and got Daddy to drive me to our restaurant the Triangle, but she had already left. Daddy and I sped down the highway to the county line, but never caught up to her. I remember crying the whole way that I needed to hug her bye. It never happened, and the next time I saw her, she was in a casket.

She had been killed in a tragic car accident while off at Georgia Southern University. Apparently, she and a bunch of friends had been out drinking and partying on a school night. Back then they had curfews, and they were racing back to the dorms that night. They were intoxicated and crashed into a pileup of several cars on a foggy highway. Mama and Daddy got the call around midnight, woke up my brother Eddie to help them with the drive, and they raced to Statesboro, which was about five hours away. At two in the morning on the drive down, Mama started crying and yelling that Deborah was dead. When they arrived at five o'clock, three hours later, the doctors told them that Deborah had died at two that morning. Even though she was more than a hundred miles away, Mama had felt her daughter's life force end. That maternal connection of a mother for her child would years later kill my mother when her son Walter ended his life.

I didn't know it then, but I graduated into an adult with adolescent tendencies after Deborah's death. At the age of twelve, I was thrust into a world of alcoholism gone wild. My parents drank and fought without fear of reprisal, my brothers went on a tangent of drugs, alcohol, and manic rages, and I was put to the task of somehow keeping Mama from working herself to death, Daddy from drinking himself to death, and despising my older brothers for not stepping up and helping me, my parents, and my little brother.

That was the first time I encountered death because of alcohol, but it would not be my last by any stretch of the imagination. Once Deborah died, everything changed within the family, and I was placed in the role of being the legitimizer of the group. I especially felt this from my parents. While they purposely removed everything in their lives that reminded them of her, they started having greater expectations for me. They actually started looking at my school report cards, they encouraged my Boy Scouts, and they put an expectation on me to be more like Deborah. It seemed that from the time of Deborah's death the entire family had me feeling a huge responsibility to live up to what she could have been. The only catch was that in being more successful, they would always resent my success as if it reminded them all of the daughter and sister they lost. It was so palatable to me that I actually calculated the exact number of days that Deborah lived, and then figured out the day that my life was to begin. The date was November 9, 1978, the day that I turned twenty years and one hundred and eleven days old. I had lasted on this earth one more day than Deborah had. I could finally start living for myself. That meant something to me, I'm just not sure why.

Howard Edward Langford Jr. AKA Eddie AKA Crazy Legs AKA Fast Eddie

December 7, 1951 - September 15, 1998

Eddie was born the first son, and the best friend of his older sister Deborah. He was a shy child who stuttered. This would lead Deborah to study child psychology at college in hopes of helping children who stuttered. Eddie started the tradition of working at an early age at the restaurant, and he was the one to get the most use of my Grandmother's skating rink. He could skate like an Olympian, and all the girls wanted to be his partner. It's my belief that the reason Eddie, my surviving brother, and I were track stars later in our lives was from our early exposure to the skating rink and the Triangle. All that skating and hopping curb at the restaurant in our youth increased our speed later on the track and football fields.

He was a good, shy, and reserved child, until he found alcohol at an early age. The gene of alcoholism had found another victim. By the time Eddie hit high school, he was well on his way to becoming a full-blown alcoholic. He was a speedster on the track and on the football field, until he got his hip broke in a game his junior year. From then on, he spent his time at the Triangle and in the bars and pool rooms with his buddies. When drugs came along in the late 1960s and early '70s, he was all in. Drugs and alcohol would lead to stories that made Eddie a folk hero of sorts, but I'm not gonna tell any of those stories now. Romancing the fun only takes away from the tragedies of Eddie's real life, which culminated in his suicide years later.

I can remember getting a toothache when I was around thirteen years old. Eddie gave me a dab of cocaine to put on the tooth to relieve the ache. I'm just glad he didn't get me to snort any of it. When Deborah died, he went off the deep end, and became the largest drug dealer in the community. It was nothing for Eddie to have a new car, three girlfriends, and cash to blow, all the while sleeping on Mama and Daddy's couch. He never recovered from losing Deborah or from the abuse of the drugs.

The earlier story of the Pinto underscores how his life was threatened by our family insanity, and how it will later give you some insight in how my family's value system was so screwed up.

If you remember the story, Eddie was busted for conspiring to sell three pounds of MDA, like the Ecstasy of the eighties, and three pounds was quite a large quantity.

When Eddie decided leave the scene at the Waffle House, the officers opened fire on the Pinto. That little car took thirty-seven bullet holes. There were shots through the door and the head rest. Three tires were shot out, and the ones in the motor finally stopped Eddie from driving off. I wish he were alive now to tell the story because it's one of the funniest stories I ever heard. He was called Clyde the entire time he was locked up, which was just over a year. He came out a changed man, but the change didn't last forever.

Eddie came out of jail, held a job for two years, and saved his money. He opened a successful deli called Daddy's Deli. He operated it until his death. The sad part is that you could visit the deli and find Eddie making sandwiches so drugged out he couldn't speak. Apparently, he found that prescription drugs and alcohol were legal, but just as lethal. Eddie had gotten into Oxycodone and Xanax and found mixing them with alcohol made the perfect trifecta.

Eddie and my little brother had a contest of sorts. They each tried to outdo the other when it came to getting into trouble with the law. Between the two of them they had over twenty DUIs and public drunkenness charges. Not only that, but they totaled over eight vehicles. However, Eddie had a few infamous "lasts" that I need to tell you about. They are his last overdose, his last DUI, and his last visit to rehab.

I'm not exaggerating when I say that Eddie was a regular at the emergency room for his overdoses. Without trying, I can think of at least six visits I made to the hospital to find him in a coma from all the prescription drugs he had taken. The last one is the most memorable because it happened so close to my little brother's suicide, and only eight days after we had buried my mother. I'll never forget walking into the hospital and being met by someone who was supposed to be my best friend. We'll call him Kevin for the sake of this story, but that's not his real name. Anyway, as I walked into the hospital, Kevin met me at the door. The funny thing is that Kevin had not supported me during any of the funerals for my father, little brother, or my mother. I guess he couldn't handle the grief, but he did nothing as far as calling me, visiting me, or supporting me during all these tragedies, and I was pissed at him for that.

I greeted him, and we walked toward intensive care. He was telling me that my brother had apparently quit breathing and could possibly have brain damage, if he survived. As we walked into the intensive care ward, I could see the room through the glass wall and saw probably six hospital employees hovering over my brother. I walked directly into the room. I walked past all the doctors and nurses who were working on Eddie. He looked terrible with all the tubes and hoses attached to him, and he was as white as a sheet. I walked straight to the head of the bed and got right up to Eddie's face. To say that I was angry would be an understatement. I started yelling at Eddie. It went something like this:

"Eddie, Eddie, Eddie, wake your ass up. If you don't wake your ass up, I promise I'm not going to give your son a damn dime from Mama's estate. WAKE YOUR ASS UP."

Believe it or not, Eddie barely opened his eyes and looked up at me. As he looked at me with those half-opened eyes, I yelled again, "You're not breathing man—the machines are doing it for you, BREATHE, MOTHEFUCKER."

He took a deep breath, and then another. I was relieved. I then yelled, "They think you have brain damage. Can you blink your eyes or something so we know you're okay?"

He blinked twice, and I told him I loved him and left the room. I had apparently dodged having another funeral. Unfortunately, I had only postponed the inevitable.

Kevin and I walked toward the hospital parking lot. I had to have a cigarette. As we're smoking outside, Kevin starts telling me how sorry he is for me, and he tells me that he's here for me. Well, that just set me off. I pulled out a piece of paper from my billfold and showed him what was on it. I had made a list of all my problems and placed my strategy for each. There was my mother, my job, my son, my little brother's estate, my plan for handling Eddie's drug choices, and my plan for handling my surviving brother who had become belligerent, threatening to attack me. I showed the list to Kevin and told him he wasn't on it. I made it clear that I knew he was not there for me; he was only there with me in the parking lot as an employee of the hospital. He was still on the clock. I asked him where the fuck he'd been during the three funerals I had had for my father, mother, and little brother. If he wanted to be here for me, he would have to do it after hours and make an effort to be a friend. I told him in no uncertain terms to kiss my ass and go back to work. That was fifteen years ago, and I haven't spoken to him since.

Eddie came out of that overdose and didn't slow down. Between the money from my mother's estate and his and his wife's addictions, he stepped up his game. It was no time before he had run through the money, lost his wife, and was living alone, isolated in a duplex all by himself. He wouldn't be long for this world from here on. It would take a couple of DUIs to move him one step closer to his death.

Before I tell you about Eddie's eleventh and twelfth DUI, let me tell you about one that he didn't get twenty years earlier. Mama and Daddy had gone to the Cotton Bowl for a University of Georgia football game. It was out in Texas somewhere, and they were gonna be gone for almost a week. Once again, I have to question their judgment as parents because they chose to leave the four of us at home alone. Not only that, but we were all living at home. There was Eddie who'd just gotten out of prison, and there was My surviving brother, who was quickly following in Eddie's footsteps. I was fifteen, full of testosterone, and Walter was only twelve. Of course, we were having a party at the house with a few of my friends. My surviving brother had a bunch of people there, and Eddie was coming over later with a bunch of people from a bar where he'd been hanging out. The house was full, and we were having a blast. A little after midnight all the lights in the house flashed off and on. We thought nothing about it and kept on partying.

Around twenty minutes later, Eddie walks in soaking wet from sweat and breathing hard. He's looking for My surviving brother, and he's frantic. He finds My surviving brother in Mama and Daddy's bedroom with his girlfriend. I follow him in there and hear Eddie telling us that he had had a wreck across town and had ran the whole way home before the police got there. Eddie's begged My surviving brother to drive back over there and take the blame for the accident. Eddie was panicked that he was about to go back to prison. Eddie promised to pay all of My surviving brother's fines, insurance premiums, and anything else he can think of at the time. My surviving brother agrees, and they drive off to get the car.

About an hour later, My surviving brother arrives back at the house alone. He comes in the door and tells us that Eddie had gotten locked up. Apparently, when they arrived, the police decided to charge My surviving brother with leaving the scene of the accident. My surviving brother explained that it was a one car accident that clipped a phone pole, and that there was no accident to have left from. Eddie, in a drunken stupor, decided to argue the case as well. The police forgot about My surviving brother leaving the scene and decided to lock Eddie up for public drunkenness. That's the Langford boy mentality at work. We can get into trouble, figure a way out, and then jump back in with both feet. It's really an inherited trait

Okay, now the story of Eddie's DUIs, number eleven and twelve. Eddie had just gotten out of the hospital for his last overdose that I was telling you about. Of course he was super man and got tagged for a DUI late on a week night. Of all the people he decided to call, he called his estranged ex-wife Barbara Ann. She obliged him and bailed him out the next morning. Apparently, they went home enjoyed each other's company, had a few drinks, and Barbara Ann decided to take Eddie to pick up his car from the impound lot. Yes, he got a DUI driving out of the impound lot. DUI's number eleven and twelve. This led him to his last rehab.

After getting bailed out for DUI number twelve, Eddie went into rehab for the last time. I can remember driving over there to see him. I drove up to into a small hospital in a small town to see my big brother in a smaller light. Eddie seemed broken. As mad as I was—and we can discuss my anger issues later—I couldn't help but feel sorry for my brother. We had a sad conversation about getting better, being a better example to his son, and the opportunities he still had to have a good life. That was the last time I ever saw him alive.

A week later, he was discharged from the hospital. He had a girl he was seeing and took a taxi to her house. Apparently, she had a pistol in the house, and he put it to his head and fired. Stupid fucking move and here's why. It was a small caliber .22 pistol, and he fired it into his temple. That's just stupid because it doesn't kill you. The bullet just bounces around your skull and turns your brain to mush. Unfortunately, I have too much knowledge on the subject because my best friend Mike would do the exact same thing with the exact same caliber pistol. Just as a sidebar, if you decide to shoot yourself, do everyone a favor, and please use a high caliber pistol, and aim to the back of the head.

Anyway, I arrived at the Winder hospital to find my brother My surviving brother in the waiting room. At least he wasn't hostile when he told me they thought Eddie was brain dead, but were transporting him to a larger hospital about forty minutes away. I was relieved when he suggested taking separate cars. It had been just over a year since he and I had spent all that time burying our little brother and our mother, and here we were again. That time didn't seem to temper My surviving brother's resentment of me, and I could feel the tension as far away as the parking lot. You'll read more about my surviving brother's and my relationship later, but it was at its worst at this point.

We arrived at the hospital around midnight, and they asked us to wait. For the first time My surviving brother and I talked about the despair. We stood there in the emergency waiting room and looked at each other with the same expression of sadness and disbelief. First, we discussed the two suicides and agreed that they didn't come from our heritage. Neither of us could remember another family member committing suicide. We then made a pact that neither of us would ever take our own life. We agreed that we had children, and for their benefit, we couldn't let them think that this was in their genes. It was really the first time I can remember talking to My surviving brother and not feeling threatened. We connected like brothers for the first and maybe the only time in my life. We both felt the shame and insanity needed to stop with our generation. Our kids were more important than we were. It didn't have to be this way for them

The doctor came out around three a.m. to tell us that the bullet had shredded Eddie's brain, and he was on complete life support. He asked us what we wanted to do. We told him to let us have our good-byes and then he could pull the plug. For the fourth time in two years, My surviving brother and I stood over our dearest family member and told them good-bye. Walter, our youngest brother, had had the good sense to finish the job, but three times we had had to make the hard and sad decision to take our loved one off life support. When the doctor and nurse came into the room to take away the life support, I left the room, but My surviving brother stayed. I just didn't have the strength, courage, or ambition to be there as I had for my mother and father. My surviving brother came out just five minutes later, and I swear he had aged ten years. He started telling me how Eddie had jerked and struggled before he expired. I knew then that I had made the right decision not to go back in.

As a side note, I should mention that my first cousin committed suicide a couple of years later. When I attended her funeral, I was standing outside smoking a cigarette with another guy there. I asked him how he knew her, and he told me he was her best friend. I explained that I was her cousin and told him about the suicides I had suffered through, and then I asked him a question.

I simply asked him who she was mad at, and what was she trying to prove? Without missing a step, he told me it was her husband. Apparently, she had often told him that she was going to kill herself, and it would he his fault. She made good on the threat one day and drove out in a field, took a bottle of Xanax, a bottle of wine, and ran a hose from the exhaust to the passenger side window and took a nap. It seems obvious to me that this generation of my family is pre-disposed to addiction and mental illness, but I don't believe we are pre-disposed to suicide. I really believe that the first two are the cause of the third. You might start off being an addict, and you might start off with a mental disability, but no human has ever started off being suicidal. It they had, they would have never made it out of being a toddler.

I guess I should add another side note to Eddie's story. It's a pretty big side note. It's about his ex-wife Barbara Ann and their son, my nephew. I hate to give the punch line away, but this story doesn't end well either.

Eddie met Barbara Ann during the heyday of his drug career, and they had a blast. She was as funny and outgoing as anyone you'd ever meet, and she knew how to party. They made a perfectly disastrous couple. Eddie would do anything, and Barbara Ann would follow, and no matter how outrageous Eddie got, she not only put up with it, she encouraged it.

It was all fun for years, but the prescription drugs hit Barbara Ann as hard as they hit Eddie. But it was crystal meth that got her killed. You see, she and Eddie had gotten divorced about a year before he died. The real cause for the divorce was the crystal meth dealer named Riley who Barbara Ann got involved with and eventually moved in with. He was apparently one mean and vicious mother fucker, and Eddie's son was stuck in the house with him.

I can only imagine what my nephew went through in that house. Although I tried getting him out of there, the court system wouldn't allow me to take him into my custody. I had always made great attempts to be an influence on Eddie's son and tried to keep him close to my son. There was more than one Christmas where I took Eddie shopping and bought his son's Santa Claus gift since Eddie and Barbara Ann had blown their money on, let's just say, other things. From the time of my divorce, when my nephew was five years old, it had become a regular thing that he would join me on my 'weekends' with my son. When my nephew turned fifteen, things had changed. I'll never forget the last time my son and I drove to pick him up. It was bad from the start.

Barbara Ann had moved from house to house after Eddie's death. They had been evicted from two or three places and had wound up out in the country just across the street from the new waste dump. It was a large house at the end of a long driveway that resembled more of a path through the woods than a driveway. As we were driving in, we were met by three kids driving a small car with a broken windshield. As we passed, we stopped to greet each other, and I asked if my nephew was home. As this punk was telling me that my nephew was in the house, I noticed a tattoo on the kid's arm. It read DUCE. I asked him what it meant, and he told me his pen name was Deuce. Since I assumed that when the guy said 'pen name' he wasn't talking about literature, but the penitentiary, I didn't mention that his tattoo was misspelled.

As we pulled up to the house, there were several cars that I didn't recognize parked all around the yard. One kid came up to the car and told me that they hadn't seen Barbara Ann for more than a week, and he was worried for my nephew. I knew this was my chance to get him out of there, and I took it. As I entered the house, I saw kids sleeping on the floor and the couch, and a few were passed out in the chairs. It looked like Peter Pan's island of lost children. There was trash everywhere, along with empty beer cans, and it smelled of a combination of rotting food, stale beer, and the inside of an ashtray. I found my nephew sleeping in the back bedroom. I woke him up and told him to get packed. We were getting out of there. I grabbed what

I could and packed my SUV with all of his stuff. We left the other kids there and drove out.

I spent most of the next week getting my nephew registered for school in my county. School had already started, but we got him registered before they had completed the first week. Once I had him settled in, I contacted Barbara Ann's sister to let her know about Barbara Ann's disappearance and to tell her where my nephew was. Her sister reported Barbara Ann missing, and it only took three days for the police to report back that Barbara Ann's body had been found.

Apparently, Barbara Ann's body had been found a couple of weeks earlier just across the Alabama/Georgia state line. Someone had shot her, taken her body across the state line, and attempted to burn her body. The local papers had been running stories on the lost woman, and the local detective there was just waiting on a report for a missing woman from Georgia that matched her description. The murderers had used an Atlanta Journal Constitution newspaper to burn her body, and the detective wasted no time when Barbara Ann was reported missing.

I got the call from the local police asking me to meet with them at my nephew's school. They were there when I arrived, and we met in a small conference room just off from the principal's office. As we sat across from each other, the two detectives brought out a large brown envelope and emptied its contents. They asked me if I recognized anything. Of course, I did.

There on the table was an assortment of my deceased mother's jewelry that Eddie had received from her estate. Mama's emerald and diamond ring, her diamond-encrusted watch, and a gold Krugerrand that she wore were lying in a pile of charred and badly burned jewelry. It was now apparently up to me to tell my nephew that his mother was dead. Like I keep saying, GOD has a high opinion of me.

The expression on my nephew's face was one of expected shock and sadness. He already knew that his mother, who doted on him constantly, wouldn't have left him unless she was already dead.

He cried, I cried, and I tried to reassure him that I was there and that we could get over this, but I knew we wouldn't. The detectives came into the room and started asking questions. My nephew had all the answers they needed to place an arrest order for Riley and track down one of the accomplices. The accomplice told them everything. The punch line here is that the accomplice was Eddie's best friend, and had actually been in Eddie and Barbara Ann's wedding. For the sake of this story, we'll call him Bill.

According to Bill, the guy Barbara Ann had moved in with had shot her and forced Bill at gunpoint to help dispose of the body. Bill got a slap on the hand and served nowhere near the time he should have. Riley ended up on the run and was finally tracked down at a state park in Alabama. Apparently, he was taking a nap in his pickup when a state ranger approached him. He shot at the ranger, a pursuit followed, and Riley holed up in some innocent bystander's home. He shot and killed himself. It was no consolation to know he was dead other than to know that he wouldn't be stalking my nephew.

It's a tragic story of depression and drug abuse and revenge that has repeated itself again and again within my family and friends. All of which has led me to having to take Eddie, Daddy, Mama, and my best friend Mike off life support. I've unplugged more people than anyone should ever have to, and then I inherited a sixteen-year-old young man with every bad habit that someone with his raising could have.

At first, my nephew blossomed while living with me. He turned sixteen, and we'd gotten him a car. Bad move on our part because, just like his dad, he totaled the car within the first month. At school, he'd made the freshman football team, and his grades were very good. He got an A in both algebra and economics. When track season rolled around, he asked me to teach him to pole vault. We worked hard, and when I wasn't available for his practice, he would record his jumps with a video camera. We would review them at night. He won his region and placed sixth in the state track meet. I thought he was on his way. Over the summer, he started running with his old crowd and reverted back to a lot of his old habits. He convinced a cousin to take over his guardianship, and he never recovered. He's been in and out of rehab numerous times, and each time I get him clean, he jumps ship. He's thirty now, and the last time I saw him, he didn't seem like he was back on track to where he should have been. As I've told him numerous times, he has a great excuse, but no reason as to why he isn't a successful young man with a family of his own.

Since my nephew is still alive, I think I'll just sum it up this way. Up to the time of my writing this, he has never recovered to be the great young man I know that he could be. The jury is still out on him though, and I keep some small ray of hope that he might someday reach his potential. My greatest wish for my nephew is that he finally gets that moment of clarity to overcome his history. It may sound counter intuitive, but I hope he gets so damn low that he truly finds a passion in life to live past his youth and that he realizes his tragedies can work to help others, and that he can enjoy the release from the insanity his parents and his uncles placed him in.

My older surviving brother

July 24, 1954 – still alive

The first memory I have in my life is of my only surviving brother almost killing me. I guess the monsters of our youth become more memorable than Santa Claus or the tooth fairy. Anyway, I'm two years old, definitely no more than two-and-a-half, (I know this because I'm still the baby of the family at this point). I'm sitting in the kitchen of our home. He is six years old at the time and is standing on a chair trying to reach the cabinet above the refrigerator. He's looking for matches. I remember the happiness on his face when he found them.

He escorts me outside where he begins to build a bonfire in the pines right behind our house. I remember trying to crawl away, but he kept picking me up and returning me within a couple of feet from the flames. The flames were hot, and I began to cry. My next memory is that of my mother and older sister Deborah running in our direction. Deborah picked me up, threw me away from the fire, and she and Mama started stomping out the flames. My older brother ran to get the hose; acting like he had just gotten there and then he blamed me for the fire. Now how in the hell does a two-year-old build a fire like that? I distinctly remember that Mama had brought an entire box of Tootsie Pops for the kids, and that I wasn't allowed to have any because they thought that I had started the fire.

Having read this little story, your first thought might be why in the hell is a six-year-old babysitting a two-year-old toddler. I write it off as just another bad job of parenting. My concern to this day is why I didn't get any damn Tootsie Roll Pops, and then why was my older brother trying to hurt me?

That's just the first of many torments my brother put me through. I remember being thrown into a steaming hot shower, having my teeth knocked out, and numerous other acts of cruelty. Besides the mental and emotional ones, I've got at least two physical scars from him as well. One is over my right eye where he pushed a gallon of pickles over the shelf, and it shattered on my head. I was maybe three-years old and came within a quarter-inch of losing my sight. The other one is when he pushed me out of the car seat of our station wagon. I had twelve stitches put in that wound. Fortunately, to this day, I still have good hair so you never see that one.

I've come to believe that he resented and was jealous of me for taking his role of being the baby of the family. Either that, or he was just plain-assed mean. Besides the other incidents of washing baby chickens in the washing machine, throwing cats off the roof to see how many flips they could do and still land on their feet, and other various acts of cruelty, he was always ready to whip my ass. I'll tell you later about my first-grade experience, but I have memories of the first grade where I didn't go to school, and instead Mama, Daddy, my older brother, and I would drive to Atlanta to visit a child psychologist. The reason they told me I was going is that he needed help. I'm starting to wonder if I was there for help as well.

My second earliest memory is of my little brother Walter being brought home from the hospital. I was two years and ten months old. The abuse from him was not a constant after that. I always thought it was because there was a new 'baby of the family' and he moved on, but now I've got a totally more realistic view of why I didn't see his wrath as often. The reason is that it's because my mother and father put his ass to work at the Triangle. He was six and that was plenty old enough in their mind to put a kid to work. I might had gotten a reprieve from his torment, but it left me always feeling intimidated by him. I think he still enjoys that fact. While we grew closer after Eddie's death, the underlying current was always one of intimidation and competition. I guess it still is.

Needless to say, he and I have had difficulties getting along for a very long time. There are far too many incidents for me to get into now. You should just assume that once I became strong enough, and fortunately that was pretty early in my life, I didn't take any more shit off of him.

Mama's major dream was for him and me to get along. Unfortunately, she never saw that in her lifetime. We did finally reconcile after Eddie's death. I mean we had to. It was down to just him and me at that point, and we needed to show our kids that this was an unacceptable way to die.

I buried all of my hostilities toward him after everybody else died, and he did the same. We got along for a few years and did a few very profitable business deals together. Unfortunately, the last one didn't start off strong (you try to start a business in 2008 and tell me how you came out), so he bailed and blamed me for the great recession. The unfortunate part is that he didn't stick with me because I eventually turned the place around, and he resents me for my success. It seems we're back to being two-and-a-half and six-years old again.

One major thing I need to say about my older brother is that he did survive all of our shit. He sobered up, married a woman who's loved him, supported him, and together they've raised their family. He worked in a manufacturing and textile plant while he built a couple of car washes and a laundromat. He's got two adult children who are better adjusted than either of us were. .He still intimidates me, but he's a hard worker and a survivor. Years ago, when I asked him how he got past all the crazy partying, and the insanity, he told me about getting on his knees and asking GOD to help him. He went on to say how he relied on the faith he received that day, and he survived. Maybe one day he and I will reconcile again, but for now it's not to be. We seem to have this unwritten agreement to just stay out of each other's lives right now. The only results from our coming together seem to be resentment, competition, and frustration. Neither of us wants to live like that.

I need to note here that this little book project has caused my brother and I to become even more estranged. While I set out to tell the entire story of my family, I made a mistake in telling his. You see, the proof copy of this book went into graphic detail of some of my older brother's adventures in his youth, and that was not for me to tell. At his request, I have taken out most references to him, except as they relate directly to me. As a result, he is referred to as "my surviving brother" in all references in this book.

You see the stigma is everywhere. We get to a place that hiding our insanities is better than the truth or in bringing them into the light. My older brother is a strong, stable man despite how he and I were raised or what we were exposed to in our genetics. His story would be much more inspirational than my scribblings, but the stigma is too strong. I hope I leave you with the impression here that my only surviving brother is a better man than I am today.

Walter Carlton Langford AKA my little brother

May 19, 1961 - July 25, 1997

Walter was my little brother and my best friend when I was small. We grew apart when I started working at the Triangle, and after Deborah's death, he never stood a chance. He and Eddie both suffered early in life with stuttering, and his only got worse after Deborah's funeral. He finally recovered from it when he found alcohol. Walter never took it well that I was concentrating on sports, work, and being a teenager and not on him. It didn't help that he had a hard time following my accomplishments on the sports field. His only way of getting any attention from Mama and Daddy was to act out in a way that brought attention. He worked hard to out party, out drink, and out do all of us when it came to acting suicidal and insane. Looking back on it, it's hard to imagine that my sweet little baby brother grew up to be a raging alcoholic and insane adult.

My first memory of Walter was when they brought him home from the hospital. I was just under three years old. We were best friends from the time he was born until Deborah died. Between me being thirteen and hitting adolescence, and being placed on the night shift at the Triangle, we grew apart.

My second memory of Walter was when he was three years old, and he had found daddy's gun. He was pointing it straight at me thinking it was a toy. Deborah came from nowhere and grabbed the gun from his hands. Thirty-three years later, while he was still living with my parents, a drunk and crazed Walter pointed a twelve-gauge shot gun at me. He didn't pull the trigger then either. My son was in the living room with us. I never took my son around Walter again, and I often went into hiding myself. Mama always let me know when Walter disappeared for more than an hour. When I got those calls, I'd leave work, sometimes leave town, and stay with friends. It was no idle threat, Walter wanted me dead.

It's sad, but after that event, whenever I visited my parents, I would rent a motel room for Walter so that my son and I could visit somewhat safely. Walter had accumulated so many DUIs that he became a convicted felon. Shortly after my father's death, Walter went on a bender, grabbed the shotgun, discharged it twice—that's thirty-nine shots fired if you're keeping count. He jumped into my father's car and told my mother that he was going to find me and kill me. Mama called the police, and Walter was sent to jail for a year. Apparently, it's illegal for a felon to discharge a firearm.

The very day he was released from prison, Walter returned to my mother's home, placed a bag over his head, ran a hose to a tank of Freon, and killed himself. Freon is the stuff you put into an air conditioner's condenser to make it cold. Walter was always smart and inventive, but he outdid himself on this one. At least he finished the job and didn't leave any of us to make the decision to unplug his ass.

The way I found out about his death was when my mother called me the next morning. I had just gotten to my office in Atlanta, when I answered the phone to hear my mother say, "Your little brother is dead. Are you happy?"

When I asked her what she was talking about, she yelled into the phone again, "YOUR LITTLE BROTHER IS DEAD. ARE YOU HAPPY?"

Mama was a little like GOD in that she put more on me than I deserved. I have to admit that while I wasn't happy, I was relieved that I wouldn't be terrorized any longer.

Walter's suicide was on July 24, my surviving brother's birthday, but the local coroner moved the suicide date to July 25 because of my surviving brother's birthday. Just two weeks later, I would have to watch my mother die when she gave up all will to live. Depending on which date you use for Walter's death, Mama lasted either sixteen or seventeen days after finding his body.

CHAPTER SIX – SUICIDE SURVIVORS

From a poem I learned in second grade:

> By the sewer I lived, by the sewer I died,
> They say it was murder, but it was sewerside.

When I was asked if I wanted to attend a suicide survivors'
meeting, I thought what a stupid idea. How in the hell do you survive
suicide? Could you not shoot straight? Didn't know how to tie a
knot? I mean, how the hell can you survive killing yourself? Who do
you blame for that?

The truth is that every successful suicide does leave survivors,
and it leaves us, in almost every case, angry with the victim. That's
the best case. The worst case is that you blame yourself and feel
guilty, and that's usually what the suicide victim wanted. If you blame
yourself for someone else taking his or her own life, then the
terrorists have won. My mother was the terrorist victim of my little
brother's suicide. Just sixteen days after he took his life, my mother,
who was not quite sixty-seven, passed away. Walter had killed her.

My oldest and youngest brothers committed suicide within
fourteen months of each other, and they both displayed the same
characteristics of withdrawal and addiction. They were allowed and
enabled to never hit their bottom, and it killed them. They withdrew
into their drug until it consumed them, and they took their lives.
When Daddy died, it started a chain reaction. My little brother

couldn't handle the loss of his daddy, Mama couldn't handle the loss of both her son and husband, and my oldest brother couldn't handle the loss of all of the above, which led to my sister-in-law being killed by her new boyfriend. And it led me to rehab and this story.

So how did I climb out of the hole? The short answer is that I hit bottom. I realized that while locked up in rehab that my greatest goal was to get into a halfway house. I don't know about you, but to me, when my life goal was to just get into a halfway house, I knew I was at the bottom. I was completely defeated, and I turned to GOD. I quit drinking with the help of rehab, Alcoholics Anonymous, and sheer determination, but I really didn't become sober until about a year later. I had started to have these panic attacks, so I went to a shrink. When I told her my history, she said that she wouldn't treat me unless I began taking several full strength psychotic prescriptions. When I resisted, she ran me out of her office. I mean she opened the door and demanded that I leave. I was completely devastated. I will never forget the feeling when I got home, and it hit me. I realized that there was no human being on this planet who could help me, and I began to pray. I asked GOD to take me and use me for whatever his will may be, and I can't begin to describe the peace and comfort that ran throughout my body and my mind. Since that day, I've strived hard to get back into society and use my talents to help others. I am the first to say that I'm not perfect in that endeavor, but I can say that there has not been a day gone by since then that I don't thank GOD for my blessings and my gifts.

If I hadn't hit my bottom, I wouldn't have given up alcohol, and if you want to help those who still suffer, you MUST help them find their bottom. To do this, you have to stop enabling them on any level, and you must over react to the insanity that addiction creates. **If insanity brings a knife, you need to pull out a gun. Your kid gets his third DUI, then you don't bail him out of jail. If your spouse says, "I'm going to commit suicide," you call the police. If they tell you they need help, then by all means drive them to rehab. The addict needs to know that they cannot get** away with their behavior anymore. **We can be there when they legitimately want to improve, but we must no longer support their poor decisions and behavior. If you do it right, it will rip your heart out. If you do this right, the addict may choose to continue using. But if you continue enabling them, they will definitely continue using, and you will lose them to their addiction.**

That is the impossible situation that the loved one of an addict faces. If you love them, you must respond in a way that may seem to harm them, and it hurts to the bone to watch them suffer for their actions. The only way you will remain sane yourself is in knowing that if you support their insanity, you are an accomplice in their death. If you behave in a way that rejects the addict and supports only their efforts to recover, then you have a shot at shocking them into a moment of clarity.

It's that moment of clarity that the addict must experience in order for them to momentarily snap out of the drug and use reason as the human being that you love so dearly. Without the addict facing some major shock to their existence, they will probably never have that moment when they can realize the drug has left them helpless. My surviving brother was fortunate enough to experience that moment while still in his early twenties. He told me of the moment he realized that he couldn't keep going. He decided to get on his knees and ask for GOD's mercy. He hit bottom and was fortunate enough and smart enough to realize it. I experienced that moment several times and chose to ignore it before I woke up in a mental hospital and was on the verge of being expelled. Neither of us would have gotten to those desperately defeated moments if our loved ones had not withdrawn their support for our addictive behaviors. It was the decision of the loved one to fight that started the process of recovery. It is the decision to fight back that results in the addict's moment of clarity. Confronting these killers is the only way to bring sanity back.

CHAPTER SEVEN – MY TURN

Gregory Milford Langford AKA Me

July 20, 1958 – Still kicking

They say that GOD doesn't put more on you than you can handle, and to put me through all of that, he must have a very high opinion of me. I think his opinion of me is way too high, but I have learned the difference between the right questions to ask and those questions that will completely drive you mad. So my first tool to suggest to you is to ask the right questions. Questions of such as:

1. What did I do to get into this and where is my action responsible?
2. What actions can I take to handle the immediate threat?
3. What actions can I take to survive the long term effects?
4. How can I turn this situation to my advantage and into a positive?

It's up to me to find the blessing in my life, and I'm still working on it. I've come to realize that anyone who lives long enough will eventually have everyone around them pass away. I just got mine a lot earlier in life than most people do, and I have a killer to pursue. I've kept the killers at bay, and I may be lucky enough to break the grip these killers have on my family. For me, the major blessing of all of the dysfunction that I experienced comes with the end result of breaking the addiction cycle for my son and future generations of Langfords. If anything positive comes from my experience, then it's that my son is a better man than I am, and with any luck, his sons will be better than both of us.

I've gone mad and returned to sanity, and that gives me a unique perspective that I'd like to share with you. When I say I went 'mad,' I mean it. I used to think that someone going 'mad' was just somebody gone crazy, but the truth is I was MAD—mad at GOD, mad at the Devil, and mad at everyone in between.

Let me make an important point here. I'm a smart guy, and I knew I was acting insane. It's a disastrous position to be there. You know your actions are not in your best interest, but you knowingly go into rages of self-righteous anger that you just can't turn away from. Unlike my brothers, I never turned suicidal, but I was as close to being homicidal as I have ever imagined that I could be. Let me tell you about a terrible day in 1998 that describes what I mean when I say I went 'mad.'

It was early November 1998, and I had just buried my oldest brother in October. Keep in mind this was the fourth funeral, the second suicide, and the third close family member who I had to unplug from life support, so you can imagine the state of frustration I was experiencing, and apparently it showed. I got a call from my sales manager telling me that he was going to take me out of my market and give it to other loan officers, and that I should just take off until the end of the year. I told him I was $15,000 shy of my annual income goal, and he agreed to pay me, if I'd just take a couple of months off. I hung up the phone mad as hell and called my wife. Her response was that she was surprised they had kept me that long, and what did I expect her to do? WELLLLLL, I said to hell with that and headed up to the north Georgia mountains to stay in a barn on a friend's farm. Now the barn had cable TV, but it was a barn nonetheless.

Here's what happened one night on the side of the mountain just outside of the barn, and this is where I can prove that I went mad. As I stood out looking over the moonlit view, it hit me that all these comparisons to Job made sense. I assume you all know the story of Job, and here's the way I saw it that night. GOD and the Devil made a bet that Job wouldn't stray from GOD if the Devil destroyed his life. GOD agreed to the bet and sicked the Devil on Job. The Devil took his family, his possessions, and struck Job down with painful boils all over his body. Job's faith never strayed from GOD, so GOD won the bet. GOD rewarded Job with multitudes of those things that he had lost.

It seemed to me that GOD and the Devil had made a bet on me. Except this time they bet that since I served neither of them, they would destroy my life and see if I followed the Devil or followed GOD.

I really did yell at the moon that night, and here is how it went:

"GOD DAMN YOU DEVIL AND DEVIL DAMN YOU GOD and fuck you Job. I'm not a pawn in your little side bet, and you're both going to lose. I ain't gonna serve either of you. Every time I do a good deed, I'm gonna do a dirty deed, and y'all can just keep me out of it. I ain't goin' to heaven, and I ain't goin' to hell, I'm gonna stay in limbo so neither of you are gonna get me. I'll tell you one thing if y'all take my son, you're gonna take me, take my kid, and you take me."

For the next twelve weeks, until I went into rehab, I went on a rampage of debauchery and sainthood. The debauchery included a lot of drinking, a lot of drugging, and a lot of mornings not knowing what I did the night before. I'm not going to get into the vivid details of what I put myself through, but to show you how bad it was, in order to balance all my Devilish deeds, I had to do so many good deeds that I became Habitat for Humanity's Man of the Year for my community. I was that deranged, and yet I've survived. I may seem wounded by others, but I'm grateful to be here, and I'm not wasting time while I'm here.

I believe that this unique experience gives me a perspective to offer you some insight as to how you can reach through to the addiction and actually get through to the person who still suffers from addiction. Having gone mad and knowing what approaches reached me, and also having the unique perspective of having been witness to so many addicts who took their own life, I think what I have to say might help you out and hopefully change a life for the better. I'm not trying to reach addicts here; I'm trying to reach their loved ones, who I believe are the unwitting accomplices in assisted suicide. It's the loved ones who are blind to the fact that by helping the addicts, they are assisting them in their addiction. It's the loved ones who blindly aid. The addict is an addict, and it's the loved one who is left as the true survivor of the addict's insanity. If you're a loved one of an addict and don't understand the addict's behavior, or know how to live in their wake, then my story is designed to speak to you. You've got a choice, just as I did, and just as every addict does, to continue behaving the same and getting the same results, or start behaving differently. It may not change the result, but it's the best you can do to fight these killers.

Okay, I'm guessing that you might think from the stories that you have a clue as to who I am. You're guess is as good as mine as to my true character and the effects of the insanity that I've shared above. The best description of me that I've ever heard was when a buddy of mine told me he thought I was an ego maniac with an inferiority complex. Before you make any final judgment, I'd like to tell you a few more stories that might shed more light on the subject.

Who's Losing Who?

First of all, my parents lost me a lot when I was a kid. They lost me at the beach when I was two; they lost me on another vacation and found their three-year-old kid alone in the pool. When I was about five years old, they left me at a movie theatre. I'll never forget the movie. It was *The Incredible Mr. Limpet* or something like that. It starred Don Knotts, famous for playing Barney Fife, as a guy who turned into a cartoon fish and helps win World War II. To this day, when I see a cartoon fish, I get nervous. My parents left me at church so many times that I used to make sure I had an extra two dimes and a nickel. I spent ten cents to call them on the pay phone at a nearby service station, ten cents on a coke, and a nickel for a pack of crackers.

To this day, I have issues with showing up on time when meeting people. I've gotten a lot better, but whenever anyone that I'm supposed to meet is running late, I start getting feelings of abandonment after about fifteen minutes. It first starts off with a sense of anticipation to be on time, then once I arrive, I immediately check the time and start questioning if I'm at the right place. If the other party is ten minutes late, my mind and body start to react. My muscles tighten, I get anxious, and I usually start to sweat. If the other party hasn't arrived after about twenty minutes, I start to reach out to them. My mind races with feelings of abandonment, resentment, and anger. I get these desperate surges of anguish. That's about the best I can describe it, but it is tangible, and it's based on Mama and Daddy forgetting me when I was a toddler.

While I'm on phobias, I might as well mention the other one of which I'm greatly aware. Strangely enough it also has to do with church, or at least with the fact that my parent's house was located immediately down the street from Winder's First Methodist Church. On Sundays when we didn't go to our own church across town, my mother would always make us come inside just before church let out at noon. She didn't want the congregation and the community to know her family wasn't at church. She put that feeling of guilt on me and probably on the rest of her kids. It would be hell stopping our play to come inside while the cars lined up at the stop sign next to our home. Each car seemed full of judgmental people dressed in their Sunday best. Even today I steer away from churches if I know it's a Sunday around noon. I currently live in a small home in a similar type neighborhood, and there's no way I'm going out of the house to be judged. Just last Sunday I was going out to my car and noticed the church crowd driving by my house. I walked out, saw the cars, and went around to the back of the house and smoked a cigarette so I couldn't be seen. After about ten minutes, I finally got into my car and drove away.

Looking back on all the times I was displaced from my family, I really can't say that they were losing me, or if I was trying to escape. I'm free now, but it's not what I expected.

My Student Athlete Career

After my mother held me back in the first grade I really didn't give education much attention. I mean I had already heard this stuff the first time I was there. For the next twelve years of school, I passed almost completely without studying. I just listened if the subject intrigued me and that was enough to get by. Fortunately, I had a couple of teachers who I liked, and I paid attention to what they were saying. As for sports, I never thought about them or had the time. While other kids were playing organized baseball, football, and such; I spent my time at the Triangle. I'm telling you these next few stories so that you can get a feeling of how enterprising my young mind was in finding tricks to survive. I may not come off as a saint here, but you'll have to admit how clever I was. I definitely had the Langford knack for getting into and out of situations using only my wits.

The school did start to separate the classes academically by the fifth grade, and all the smart kids were in the A group. For some reason, I was placed in there. After Deborah's death, I got put back into the B group for the second half of school. During the seventh grade, a teacher noticed I was sleeping all during his second period history class and still making straight As. He approached me and asked if I was bored with the material. It was history, so who ain't bored with that subject? I told him I was bored just to make him happy. I didn't have the heart to tell him that I'd closed down the restaurant the night before and didn't get home 'til eleven o'clock. I also didn't have the gumption to tell him I'd gotten all the test answers from a girl who took first period. He put me back in A group.

We also had a geometry class during the seventh grade where we had to build a geometric design with string on a piece of wood. I ain't handy and never met a hammer or nail that I liked. So using a piece of hippy art that had been given to my oldest brother, I took off the string and painted the board a different color. I not only got an A for the project, but a ribbon, too, and they displayed it in the library. About twenty years ago, someone told me it was still there. That means it was on display for twenty-five years after I painted it. How's that for a legacy?

I'll quit with the stories on school after this last one. When I was a senior, I had convinced my dad to pay for a student trip to Europe. It was $1,000 in 1976 and that wasn't no chump change back then. The teacher heading the trip was a beautiful Greek Goddess, and she was excited that I was going along. One day another teacher caught me hooking out of class and returning to drop off a friend. The guy approached me and said "I got you this time, Langford, leaving school property during school hours will get you suspended." I told him I was moving chairs for the Greek Goddess, and he could verify it with her. I coolly walked to the door of the hall and took off running as fast as I could. I arrived in her class and told her what I'd done, and if she didn't back me, then there was no way my dad would let me go to Europe. (That was a lie, my dad would have thought it was funny.)

Just after telling her this, the other teacher walked up and asked her to meet with him in the teacher's lounge. About three minutes later, the guy walks out, red-faced, and looking pissed. Apparently, the Greek Goddess had covered my story, and Europe was a blast.

The teacher who had caught me was a bitch from then on. He was giving us a final, and he smiled as he told me that I'd have to make an A if I expected to get a C in the class. No sweat for me. You see, I had this other friend who had lost his mother to cancer, and his father was a disaster as a parent. The school offered my friend a job cleaning the entire school to help out the family. In addition, to him and me running the hallways and shooting basketball in the gym at night, he also had keys to all of the teachers' homerooms. He opened the door to the room I needed, and I rifled through the teacher's desk, found the tests, and I made the A. I made a 92 on purpose. I figured he might get wise to me if I scored a 100.

On the athletics' side, I did finally try to play football when I was thirteen. I had played a lot of backyard ball, but my work schedule at the Triangle never allowed me to play organized football. After three or four practices, I was tearing up the field as a running back. After one practice, I rode my bike to the Triangle, and my mom was there. She was working my shift, and I couldn't stand the guilt I felt for her having to work so that I could pursue football. I quit football before the first game, and went back to work. I didn't play again until high school. I was the starting running back, and in the three years I played, my mom only saw one game. Friday nights were our busiest nights at the restaurant, and she couldn't leave. I remember the game she saw me play was an away game against Norcross High School. I had three runs of over thirty yards and one touchdown called back because one of the guards kept holding. I threatened to kick his ass after the third holding call. I ended up with only a few official yards and no touchdowns. We won the game, but I was crying outside the locker room because I wanted my mom to see me score. The coach came up to me, got in my face, and started yelling that we'd won, and that I wasn't a team player because I was crying about my performance. He can kiss my ass to this day. I wasn't crying because of my low numbers, I was crying that my mama didn't get to see me shine. The feeling of completely letting her down was too much for me to contain.

It was the track team where I really excelled. My freshman year, I was the fastest guy on the team. I anchored the first team all year until the regional meet. That's when the coach told me he was running all seniors on the first team, and I was demoted to the second team. At the finals, my team came in third, but the first team came in fourth. I was running the last leg, and when I got the baton I was a strong ten yards behind the senior on the first team. I couldn't catch the rest of the teams, but caught his ass and passed him at the finish line. The coach gave me a letter but no jacket. I guess he can still kiss my ass as well. That little incident re-enforced my feeling of inadequacy and contributed to my lack of respect for authority figures. Fortunately, that coach quit and two new mentors entered my life as track coaches.

My sophomore year, we got a new coach and one who had his act together. He recruited anyone not on crutches, and we started a dynasty that lasted more than twenty years at my school. This coach made us set goals, required us to work every day, and showed us how to be winners. It was the first time I was exposed to real structure and an outline for being a winner, and one that I carry until this day. We won the state track championship my senior year, and I was one of the captains. We won by the six points I scored in the pole vault. I never felt as victorious as I did at that moment and then later with all the accolades the school laid on us after we won. That coach saved my ass.

When I went on to college, I laid away my athletics but applied those skills toward my approach to my education. I set a goal every quarter, studied every day, did my research at night, and got out of school with a 3.13 GPA. Not bad for someone who finished one hundred out of two hundred with a C average in high school. I also drove home every Friday after my last class and worked the Triangle 'til one in the morning. Then I worked all Saturday and half a day Sunday so Mama could get some rest.

I was bored during the week my freshman year and decided when the spring came to grab my old pole and walk onto the track team just for something to do. I ended up getting a scholarship at a junior college close to home for one quarter. I set their pole vault record in 1978, and they cancelled the track program after that year. So, I still hold the pole vault record to this day. The point of telling you my sports history is to underscore how someone outside of the family can be a positive influence on a young man. The habits I gained in sports of having a written plan, setting goals, working everyday toward that goal, and applying myself are what helped me to survive. I bet I'm the only guy you know who has a written action plan on how to handle insanity. All I can say is that it seems to work for me.

My Two Longest Relationships

After my mother held me back in the first grade I really didn't give education much attention. I mean I had already heard this stuff the first time I was there. For the next twelve years of school, I passed almost completely without studying. I just listened if the subject intrigued me and that was enough to get by. Fortunately, I had a couple of teachers who I liked, and I paid attention to what they were saying. As for sports, I never thought about them or had the time. While other kids were playing organized baseball, football, and such; I spent my time at the Triangle. I'm telling you these next few stories so that you can get a feeling of how enterprising my young mind was in finding tricks to survive. I may not come off as a saint here, but you'll have to admit how clever I was. I definitely had the Langford knack for getting into and out of situations using only my wits.

The school did start to separate the classes academically by the fifth grade, and all the smart kids were in the A group. For some reason, I was placed in there. After Deborah's death, I got put back into the B group for the second half of school. During the seventh grade, a teacher noticed I was sleeping all during his second period history class and still making straight As. He approached me and asked if I was bored with the material. It was history, so who ain't bored with that subject? I told him I was bored just to make him happy. I didn't have the heart to tell him that I'd closed down the restaurant the night before and didn't get home 'til eleven o'clock. I also didn't have the gumption to tell him I'd gotten all the test answers from a girl who took first period. He put me back in A group.

We also had a geometry class during the seventh grade where

we had to build a geometric design with string on a piece of wood. I ain't handy and never met a hammer or nail that I liked. So using a piece of hippy art that had been given to my oldest brother, I took off the string and painted the board a different color. I not only got an A for the project, but a ribbon, too, and they displayed it in the library. About twenty years ago, someone told me it was still there. That means it was on display for twenty-five years after I painted it. How's that for a legacy?

I'll quit with the stories on school after this last one. When I was a senior, I had convinced my dad to pay for a student trip to Europe. It was $1,000 in 1976 and that wasn't no chump change back then. The teacher heading the trip was a beautiful Greek Goddess, and she was excited that I was going along. One day another teacher caught me hooking out of class and returning to drop off a friend. The guy approached me and said "I got you this time, Langford, leaving school property during school hours will get you suspended." I told him I was moving chairs for the Greek Goddess, and he could verify it with her. I coolly walked to the door of the hall and took off running as fast as I could. I arrived in her class and told her what I'd done, and if she didn't back me, then there was no way my dad would let me go to Europe. (That was a lie, my dad would have thought it was funny.)

Just after telling her this, the other teacher walked up and asked her to meet with him in the teacher's lounge. About three minutes later, the guy walks out, red-faced, and looking pissed. Apparently, the Greek Goddess had covered my story, and Europe was a blast.

The teacher who had caught me was a bitch from then on. He was giving us a final, and he smiled as he told me that I'd have to make an A if I expected to get a C in the class. No sweat for me. You see, I had this other friend who had lost his mother to cancer, and his father was a disaster as a parent. The school offered my friend a job cleaning the entire school to help out the family. In addition, to him and me running the hallways and shooting basketball in the gym at night, he also had keys to all of the teachers' homerooms. He opened the door to the room I needed, and I rifled through the teacher's desk, found the tests, and I made the A. I made a 92 on purpose. I figured he might get wise to me if I scored a 100.

On the athletics' side, I did finally try to play football when I was thirteen. I had played a lot of backyard ball, but my work schedule at the Triangle never allowed me to play organized football. After three or four practices, I was tearing up the field as a running back. After one practice, I rode my bike to the Triangle, and my mom was there. She was working my shift, and I couldn't stand the guilt I felt for her having to work so that I could pursue football. I quit football before the first game, and went back to work. I didn't play again until high school. I was the starting running back, and in the three years I played, my mom only saw one game. Friday nights were our busiest nights at the restaurant, and she couldn't leave. I remember the game she saw me play was an away game against Norcross High School. I had three runs of over thirty yards and one touchdown called back because one of the guards kept holding. I threatened to kick his ass after the third holding call. I ended up with only a few official yards and no touchdowns. We won the game, but I was crying outside the locker room because I wanted my mom to see me score. The coach came up to me, got in my face, and started yelling that we'd won, and that I wasn't a team player because I was crying about my performance. He can kiss my ass to this day. I wasn't crying because of my low numbers, I was crying that my mama didn't get to see me shine. The feeling of completely letting her down was too much for me to contain.

It was the track team where I really excelled. My freshman year, I was the fastest guy on the team. I anchored the first team all year until the regional meet. That's when the coach told me he was running all seniors on the first team, and I was demoted to the second team. At the finals, my team came in third, but the first team came in fourth. I was running the last leg, and when I got the baton I was a strong ten yards behind the senior on the first team. I couldn't catch the rest of the teams, but caught his ass and passed him at the finish line. The coach gave me a letter but no jacket. I guess he can still kiss my ass as well. That little incident re-enforced my feeling of inadequacy and contributed to my lack of respect for authority figures. Fortunately, that coach quit and two new mentors entered my life as track coaches.

My sophomore year, we got a new coach and one who had his act together. He recruited anyone not on crutches, and we started a dynasty that lasted more than twenty years at my school. This coach made us set goals, required us to work every day, and showed us how to be winners. It was the first time I was exposed to real structure and an outline for being a winner, and one that I carry until this day. We won the state track championship my senior year, and I was one of the captains. We won by the six points I scored in the pole vault. I never felt as victorious as I did at that moment and then later with all the accolades the school laid on us after we won. That coach saved my ass.

When I went on to college, I laid away my athletics but applied those skills toward my approach to my education. I set a goal every quarter, studied every day, did my research at night, and got out of school with a 3.13 GPA. Not bad for someone who finished one hundred out of two hundred with a C average in high school. I also drove home every Friday after my last class and worked the Triangle 'til one in the morning. Then I worked all Saturday and half a day Sunday so Mama could get some rest.

I was bored during the week my freshman year and decided when the spring came to grab my old pole and walk onto the track team just for something to do. I ended up getting a scholarship at a junior college close to home for one quarter. I set their pole vault record in 1978, and they cancelled the track program after that year. So, I still hold the pole vault record to this day. The point of telling you my sports history is to underscore how someone outside of the family can be a positive influence on a young man. The habits I gained in sports of having a written plan, setting goals, working everyday toward that goal, and applying myself are what helped me to survive. I bet I'm the only guy you know who has a written action plan on how to handle insanity. All I can say is that it seems to work for me.

Visits to the Cemetery

You can learn a lot about a family's history by driving through an old cemetery. Just by surveying each plot, it's easy to figure out how rich the family was, how long the parents lived, how many children never lived long enough to survive the parents, what times they lived and died in, and whether or not they were in the military.

I hate to drive through Rose Hill Cemetery in my home town of Winder. I grew up there, my father was a city councilman and mayor there for thirty years, and I've got not one, but two resolutions honoring him for his service from the Georgia Legislature. My mother's family's name was Harris, and her family tree can be traced back to William Henry Harris, who served in the Continental Army under Washington at Valley Forge. He was from Virginia and moved to Georgia on a land grant around 1783.

I've traveled quite a bit and have come to learn that not every culture handles their dead in the same manner. All I can say is that in Georgia, we put cemeteries anywhere we please. You'll be driving around, and you'll see cemeteries side by side with school playgrounds, in the middle of subdivisions, and beside every little church or chimney from a burned-out church and almost anywhere else we decided to honor our dead.

Driving through Rose Hill toward my family plot, I recognize quite a bit of the other families' histories, as I drive up to my own. Each plot measures roughly thirty feet by thirty feet, is trimmed in auburn brick foundations, and is filled with little white rocks. Each plot has a family headstone, and the footstones tell the stories of who lies there.

Rose Hill is built on hills with crisscrossing roads leading to each dead end. (I couldn't help myself on that one). Daddy bought the lot in the late '60s. He and Mama chose a nice corner lot in Rose

Hill because it overlooked the high school, and the football field, and you could see Mama's church, the First Christian Church from there. You could see those landmarks in the '60s, but the view was blocked in the early 2000s during the residential real estate boom. That's when they built Rose Hill Apartments right on the property line. Now, the residents of the cemetery have a great view of the back of these apartments and the parking lot of the tenants. Apparently, in the south, we not only build cemeteries next to anything, but we'll build anything next to a cemetery.

Each time I drive through there—and I'll be the first to admit that I don't visit often—I pay particular attention to the other plots' footstones. You see a whole lot of two footstones, I call them 'twosies,' and after reading quite a few, I've noticed it's mainly because of married couples who died after years together, and either had no children or the kids were buried elsewhere. My census of the dead reveals very few 'onesies,' a bunch of 'twosies' and 'threezies,' and a couple of 'foursees.' I notice all this as I drive up to my five footstone family plot. Each plot is measured twenty feet by twenty feet, and there's just enough room for five burial sites. I know Georgia has a law that says you can only marry the same woman five times, then after that it's against the law to marry the woman again. I wonder if Rose Hill adopted the same rule for its burial sites. It's a shame there's not enough room for me, but then again, I never did fit in with my family.

As you survey the Langford plot, you'll notice from left to right, my sister Deborah who passed away at the age of twenty in 1970 when I was twelve, my father Howard Edward Langford, Sr. who passed away in 1996 when I was thirty-seven, my mother Irene who died in 1997 when I was thirty-eight, my little brother Walter who died in 1997 when I was thirty-eight, and my oldest brother Howard Edward Langford, Jr. (Eddie) who died in 1998 when I was thirty-nine.

It's tough to see them all together like this, especially considering how poorly we all got along when they were alive. I've got my dead sister who I missed telling good-bye, my father who I couldn't allow to die in dignity, my mother who died of a broken heart, my little brother whose greatest goal in life had been to torment me and see me dead, and my oldest brother who left me the shambles of his broken family and his son who could have used a better example to follow. I don't enjoy the reunion at the gravesite, but I go anyway.

I usually begin with telling everyone hello. I start with Deborah and am immediately overcome with guilt and remorse that she didn't live longer. I really believe that if she hadn't died in that car wreck, then our family would have had a different and more positive dynamic.

I then move to Daddy and bring him up to date on my personal and business problems. He was always my mentor when it came to making major life decisions. I'm not saying I always took his advice, but I always sought his guidance. When Deborah died, I felt I'd let her down, but when Daddy died, I felt that I'd lost my safety net. Once he was gone, I was truly on my own, just as if life was a tight rope act, and if I fell then I'd hit the ground if he wasn't there to back me up. Talking to his headstone feels surreal; the whole trip seems like a bad dream or terrible suppressed memory coming back into light. It's embarrassing, hair raising, and incredibly solemn. The feeling that comes over my body is palatable. I feel dirty, as if I need a shower to wash off the complete cloud or fog of dysfunction that has attached to my body.

After spending a moment with Daddy, I move right to Mama's stone, and my emotions move to one of total loss. I really miss my mother, and I tell her so. I start talking to her headstone and bring her and Daddy up to date on how my son is doing, who I'm currently married to, how their other grand kids are doing, and then I usually just sit there in silence for a few minutes. There's not much more to say to her.

It would be great if I could just have those three conversations and hit the road, but that's not the way it usually works out. If I had the temperament to just walk away with the feeling of loss for Deborah, Daddy, and Mama, it would be similar to what I think other people experience when they visit their loved ones in a graveyard, but that ain't my temperament, and I move to the right to speak to Walter and Eddie. That's usually when my temper comes out.

When I get to Walter, what do I say? I've written letters to him posthumously saying I forgive him, but I don't. I've tried to tell his tombstone that I understand that he was sick, and I couldn't be mad at someone who had the flu, so I should forgive him for being sick, but I don't. Imagine how you would feel if the person who killed your mother was your brother, and that their footstones lay side by side. Every time I visit my mother's grave, I have to visit her killer's grave as well. That's just fucked up. It's not easy visiting one without being reminded of the other. I can honestly say that I've forgiven him for his treatment of me because I have, but I just can't get beyond the fact that his suicide caused my mother's death. My usual comment to his tombstone is a quick "FUCK YOU," and then I move again to my right.

Then there's Eddie. Poor ole Eddie. I feel a combination of anger, sadness, and disappointment when I get to Eddie. I usually tell him what a fuckin' mess he left and get even more pissed off. I had to tell him the love of his life was murdered by her boyfriend because he couldn't step up. I bring him up to date on his son, which gets me more aggravated because his son didn't deserve to lose both his father and his mother. At that point, I usually take a few steps backwards so that I can speak and take in the entire group.

It's not too rare for me to be talking aloud to these granite blocks. More often than not, I end up raising my voice and using a lot of profanity. I tell Mama, Daddy, and Deborah good bye, but I tell Walter and Eddie "Fuck you," and drive away sad, angry, betrayed, and abandoned. Each time I visit that place, I promise myself that I won't come back, but then I feel guilty that I don't visit enough. It's a strange battle I've faced with my family since I was a little kid.

I seem to make these trips with less and less frequency; it's just too emotional, and I don't find any comfort in visiting there. I've made a will, which states that when I die, I'm not to be buried there, but that my ashes are to be spread into a local river which travels through Athens, the University of Georgia, and then down to the Atlantic Ocean. My ass might not have been able to escape this place, but my ashes can.

There was one time when as I was getting back into my car that I distinctly heard my mother's voice say sharply, "And get a damn haircut." I returned a couple of days later with my ears lowered.

Rose Hill Cemetery – the Langfords
From left, Deborah, Daddy, Mama, Walter, Eddie

The Langfords
From left – Barbara Ann (Eddie's wife who was murdered), Me
(holding my wild son), Mama (who died of a broken heart), Eddie's son
(orphaned by suicide of father and murder of mother), Daddy, another
grandson, Eddie (suicide one year after Walter), and Walter (suicide at
Mama's causing her heartbreak).

The Historic Jackson Building

Just before my mother passed away, I had purchased a five-story building on the square in Gainesville, Georgia. When it was originally built in 1908, it was the tallest building between Atlanta and Asheville, North Carolina. There were retail stores on the first floor, the second floor held corporate offices, and the top three floors held sixteen apartment units. The building towers over the main square of the town.

Shortly after my oldest brother's suicide and losing my job, I moved out of the house that I shared with my second wife, and moved into the Jackson Building. The best part is that there were two great bars and a couple of restaurants, and I was still drinking. In addition to all that, I had fifteen tenants who liked to party as well. The stage was set for my demise.

I had ambition back then to become eccentric. Despite all of my personal issues, my banking career had been successful, and I had purchased a couple of real estate properties that provided a decent cash flow. If I leveraged it right, I could have a pretty good living without really working. I could be focused on crazy and have enough money to live. By my definition, the only difference between a mad man and an eccentric is that the eccentric has money. Since I had already condoned myself to the fact that I was crazy, I might as well enjoy myself.

My first step was to remodel half of the top floor, making myself a large apartment. I put a huge Christmas tree on top, and while they were lifting the tree, I hauled enough lumber up there for a great wooden deck on the roof, and I remodeled the basement as a combination office and pool room.

The only problem was that my pool table was still at my wife's house. I was mentioning this to a worker, and he told me that "If you lead the calf, the cow will follow," and that I just needed my stepdaughter to want something else in our basement at the house. The next day on a visit to the house, I suggested to my stepdaughter that I could get her a ping pong table if she liked. I got permission from her mom that night to move the pool table, and I was set.

During all this time, my second wife had continually tried to get me to move back home, and she refused a divorce. For some crazy reason, she didn't want to let me go regardless of how I insane I'd gotten. I had to leave her though. It wasn't fair to pull her down with me. She was trapped in the real world and was very successful; I was trapped in a mental insanity that was waging war on the world and its creator. Regardless of this, she wouldn't let go. This caused me to come up with a diabolical plan to get her to want me to leave. Remembering the old adage 'lead the calf and the cow will follow," I decided to move back home with her and behave so badly that it would be her idea that we divorce. My plan was to take two Xanax, smoke a couple of joints, and get drunk every night. My assumption was that she would get tired of me passing out every night and kick me out. The plan backfired, and I ended up in a mental ward a few weeks later.

CHAPTER EIGHT - REHAB

I've been asked several times what finally convinced me to go to rehab, so I'll tell you. The short answer is that I felt completely defeated. Nothing was working for me. I'd lost my job, I was living in the Jackson Building, and with all the deaths, I felt as isolated and angry as a person could be. So I moved back home and implemented my plan.

After about three weeks of my plan being put into play, I arrived at my home where my second wife, unbeknownst to me, had invited my best friend to hold an intervention. It was late on a Friday night, and I staggered into the house only to find my best female friend Tammy sitting in the living room. They confronted me as I came into the house. I had already drank at least a six pack and taken a Xanax before I arrived, and I'm sure the smell of marijuana surrounded me.

The conversation started with them both telling me that they loved me, but I needed help. Tammy started tearing up as she told me how much I meant to her, that I was valuable, and that she didn't want me to end up like Eddie and Walter. A rush of embarrassment came over me like an emotional waterfall, and I wanted to crawl into hole, but instead I slashed back with a torrent of "I ain't gonna kill myself, I don't need no help." I raged, asking who was she to judge me. Tammy stood up and told me that I needed help and that they had already lined up a rehab center for me. She started telling me how terribly bad I looked and how much she was worried about me. I got in her face and reminded her that I'd just gotten high with both her and her husband just the week before. She told me that I looked like shit, and I told her that her ass was fat. She wouldn't back down, and I gave up. The bravado was gone, and a sense of complete hopelessness came over me. While I gave in to seeking help, in the back of my mind, my pride kept telling that if I just consented to these women and ended this argument, I'd get out of it somehow.

It was roughly ten o'clock on a Friday night, so I told them to make the call. I thought the place would be closed, but guess what, rehab centers are like Waffle Houses in that they are open twenty-four hours a day. Who knew? As they got the front desk on the phone, I told them to make sure that they knew I was drunk and stoned. I thought they didn't take people who were high. Guess what, rehab centers take drunks. I was screwed. I vaguely remember the hour and a half drive to the hospital, but I distinctly remember being curled up in the fetal position, kinda halfway on the floor board and on the front passenger seat as my second wife drove us the hour and a half.

As we turned into the Ridgeview Mental Center, we entered a long driveway, which opened up to a large complex of buildings scattered around a large campus. I remember how quiet the place was as we got out of the car around midnight. The lobby looked just like any large waiting room, with a few people sitting quietly, and I felt a paranoia that they all knew my name and what I was there for. My wife signed us in at the window, and I flopped into a cold leather chair and waited. They called us in, took all my insurance documents—back then insurance actually paid for mental health costs—and sat us back in the lobby.

After what seemed like an eternity, these two large white doors opened, and a huge, and I mean huge, nurse came out to invite me in. Once those big doors closed behind me, I felt both a panic and a calmness that kept sweeping back and forth within me. I knew I was going to get help or die, and I was scared shitless. I followed her down this long hospital corridor, head down, feet dragging, and emotionally wore out.

These other doors opened, and I'm standing in the lobby for the rehab ward. This is where the mentally ill and the addicts are segregated from the main hospital. It had the look of my old college dorm lobby with a large lobby, a separated television room, and a few tables sitting around. There was absolutely no one in the lobby but a nurse or two. I was told that all the rooms were taken for the night and that I'd have to sleep in the main area on a cot until they could get me a bed the next day. I staggered over to this little cot with one pillow and a blanket on it, stripped down to my underwear, and passed out on the cot. I woke up to one of the strangest mornings I've ever experienced.

Consciousness returned to me the next morning in the form of coming to rather than waking up. I opened my eyes that morning to a bustling lobby that had the feel of a hospital without the smell of formaldehyde and death that I usually smelled in hospitals. There were around twenty people shuffling around wearing paper socks, another ten or so lined up at the med window, while wearing their pajamas, and maybe another ten people watching TV in a little room off to the side. My first thought was that that I had somehow been transformed into the movie *One Flew Over the Cuckoo's Nest*. That's the only way I can describe the scene. It took a second or two, but I started remembering what I'd done the night before and that I had apparently stripped down before passing out. I was laying there almost naked with all these people wandering around, and I had to get dressed. As I stood up and put my clothes on, I felt a little self-conscious, but as I looked around, it became acutely clear that nobody paid me a bit of attention.

A young male counselor informed me that I was in the lock up ward for now but was free to leave. If I left, I couldn't come back, but I could check out at any time. I was to meet my doctor in the afternoon, and he would assign me to the on-campus halfway house.

He then told me to get into the line for meds. Before I did that I found a pay phone—yes, they still existed in 1999—and called my last surviving brother. I remember as I was dialing his number that I was uncertain about what to tell him. Once he answered, I started off by telling him a joke about not having a belt or shoe laces and that I was in rehab. Believe it or not, that's not an unusual call for either him or me to get. We'd gotten so many of these calls from Eddie and Walter that we took them in stride. The unusual part is that I was making the call. He volunteered to come get me, but in a moment of clarity, I told him no. The truth was that I'd been trying to get help from doctors, psychiatrists, churches, and prayers and none of it had worked. I figured this might be my last chance. With more than a little bravado, I told him that.

I told him my plan was to stick around for a few days but for him to be ready to come get me if I decided to 'break out.' I hung up the phone and anxiously awaited the meeting with my doctor, which was a story in and of its self.

It was a Saturday afternoon, and I'd spent the day meeting my fellow inmates. They all seemed to possess a very wide variety of ailments. There were people drugged out in wheelchairs, people shuffling from one point to the other talking to themselves, people passed out on their meds in the TV room, and what seemed like regular guys and a lot of attractive, younger, thin women. There was also the occasional yelling and screaming from time to time.

I was told that my doctor wouldn't be able to see me until Sunday, the next day. That's also why the inmates weren't in their normal 'sessions.' Someone explained that I couldn't get out of this ward and into a halfway house until I was evaluated by the shrink. I was pissed that I'd have to stay another night with the insanity ward. The next day when I met with my assigned shrink for the first time, I was mad at him before I met him.

I walked in with my cocky attitude and met the most arrogant man I've ever met. It was like looking into a mirror. This guy was just as cocky as I was and acted so superior that I had an immediate dislike for his ass. Apparently, the feeling was mutual, and it wasn't long before we got off track. When I asked him his name, he told me that we weren't going to get into a personal relationship and that he was smarter than I was. My retort was to tell him that he might be the boss here, but if we were dropped on a desert island, he'd be my bitch in two weeks. The man told me that I could leave at any time. That hit home with me and scared me to the core. It's that 'moment of clarity' that had allowed me to make a lucid decision on my way of life. I was at my most vulnerable, my bravado and ego had failed me, and I was willing to listen. This man threatening to take away his support was enough to shock me into reality, if even for a short period of time. I didn't want to keep going the way I was living and rejecting this man's help seemed like a terrible decision. I decided to listen, argue, fuck with his head a little, and settle down. It's said that an addict gets to choose his bottom, and I chose this one. As I sat there and evaluated my position, it was obvious that I had bottomed out. In my mind, being in a place in life where my greatest goal was to get out of an insanity ward and into a halfway house was a pretty low point. If this wasn't my bottom, I might die. We set another appointment for Monday, and I left for my first Alcoholics Anonymous (AA) meeting.

As I left the session, I immediately asked one of the nurses the doctor's name. If he didn't want me to know his first name, I wanted to prove that I was smart enough to get it myself. The nurse responded immediately with a name. We'll just call him Dr. Robert Carson for our purposes, but I had a little ammunition for our next meeting. He showed his opinion of our meeting by not transferring me to the halfway house until Monday. I was stuck in the 'Cuckoo's nest' for another two days. The game was on.

I was transferred to the halfway house early Monday morning before I was to meet my shrink, the good doctor Carson. One of the guys in the halfway house told me that he knew the good doctor from having been in rehab several years earlier. It seems that my shrink was once an anesthesiologist and got hooked on the gas. He was here earlier as a patient and apparently changed professions from anesthesiologist to psychiatrist. He was pretty smart after all. My inmate also tells me the guy is Jewish. I was loaded for bear at our next meeting. I couldn't be sure of the source, but I ran with the information anyway

He calls me into his office, and I immediately pop off, "What's happening, Bobby?" He knows I have his name. He asks me how I'm doing, and I play upon his ego by telling him I had a lot of bad dreams the night before and even had one about him. Of course, he wants to hear about the dream he's in, so I tell him:

I'm in this surgery room, and I'm strapped down on the table. Everyone there is wearing green scrubs, and he's there as well, only he's wearing a pink scrub. I tell him that he's holding his mask like he's the anesthesiologist, but I act as if I can't remember how to say it. With that, I've gotten him to say anesthesiologist instead of me. I then tell him that just before he was placing the mask on me, he took the mask and placed it on to his own face and inhaled deeply. He then looked at me lying on the table, took the mask off, and said to me "Shalom."

Now tell me who's the smart one, the one telling the story or the one who's frantically writing in his little book? He never looked up as he made his notes on those pages, but his demeanor changed. I'm a master of body language, and I smiled as I watched him squirm in his chair, and he scrunched his brows. I guarantee you the good doctor was calling his own shrink after that session. I quit fucking with him after that and began pursuing sobriety in a serious manner. I had picked up a white chip of surrender from the AA meeting the day before, and my head was clearing. I'd never surrendered before, I had always had to fight. The feeling that the only way to beat my addiction to alcohol was to give up overcame me. If I give up and surrender, I win. It became that simple. Not easy, but simple.

He and I eventually became adjusted to each other, and he really helped me a lot. The most important thing he ever did for me was telling me that first day that I could leave at any time, forcing me to make my own decision to stay for help.

On our last visit, I told him that I had thought about bringing a couple of IQ tests for us to take to see who really is smarter. His response was that if I had brought them, I would find out that he is smarter. My response to that was that he would have found out that I had already opened mine and found the answers. Again, I ask who is smarter?

The Miracle of Alcoholics Anonymous

I know I casually mentioned Alcoholics Anonymous earlier, but they really deserve their own book. Oh yeah, they have one, and it saved my life. I can honestly say that prior to being introduced to AA, I had tried every spiritual remedy that I could have thought of or that was suggested to me. I tried shrinks, religion, meditation, and read any written material I could find. None of them came close to saving my soul the way Alcoholics Anonymous did. I picked up my first white chip—the surrender chip—and thus far, have never taken another drink. Only Alcoholics Anonymous worked for me.

There's a couple of things you need to know about AA. One is that it was called Anonymous because the first groups were afraid that their members would be overridden with requests for help should they not remain anonymous. The second thing is that one of the suggestions is that none of its members brag in the public's eye about being a member for fear that person 'go out' and drink again; it would look bad on us all. With that said, may I suggest only that if you or a loved one are suffering from addiction, please look into a local AA meeting. The ability to talk and interact with other addicts is truly amazing. They don't judge you because they've lived it themselves. It's not like going to a shrink and paying someone to hear you bitch while they try to figure you out. It's not like going to a church and feeling as if GOD and the priest are judging your soul. Spending time with other recovering addicts is like a spiritual release. You can tell a recovering alcoholic that you shot your wife, had sex with a gorilla, and robbed a bank yesterday and their only question is

"Did you drink over it?" There is no judgement at all, and that formula worked for me. I practice their program to this day, but I'll never forget my first AA meeting outside of rehab.

When I was released from rehab, one of the first things I did was to reach out to one of my oldest friends who had just gotten sober a few months earlier. Mike and I met on a high school spring break in Daytona Beach when I was a senior and he was a freshman. I had known his older brother Ray who had passed away in a car wreck just a couple of years earlier. Ray was still a teenager when he died. Even though I was eighteen and he was only fourteen, Mike and I hit it off from the start. I was impressed by his sense of humor and his ability to party. This kid could hang with the best of us and we kind of took him under our wings. After that high school trip, Mike and I became very close friends, and all during my college career, we partied together and supported each other. After college, his wife Tammy and my first wife were fast friends, and we continued to party while we grew our families. He was truly one of my best friends, and I loved him. By the way, it was Mike's wife Tammy who came to my home a few months earlier and talked me into going to rehab.

When I contacted Mike after I got out of rehab, he had about three months' sobriety and was going to at least one AA meeting a day. I could tell he wasn't too happy to hear from me. For the past several months, I'd reached out to him late at night in a drunken stupor. I didn't know it at the time, but he had already found his bottom and was working to stay sober. My calls apparently didn't help. I didn't call Mike when I got out of rehab, I drove to his house, but he wasn't home. I remember thinking how desperately scared I was and confused about what to do as I waited in my car until he finally arrived from work. He got out of his car, and you could tell he wasn't overjoyed to see me.

His attitude changed shortly into the conversation after I told him that I'd just gotten out of rehab and needed to find a meeting. I asked him if he could take me to a couple of AA meeting locations and be my 'sponsor.' Mike's response shocked me. He firmly and point blank told me that his sobriety was the most important thing to him, and that I wasn't gonna fuck that up. He would take me to two meetings that night, but after that I was on my own. It would be completely up to me to return to meetings, and to find my own sponsor. I saw his sincerity and respected that. I also knew he wasn't going to support me if I wasn't serious. He was quite content to allow me to find my bottom if this wasn't it. That was exactly what I needed hear. His telling me that he loved me but wasn't gonna support me if I wasn't committed to change reinforced my fear and determination. It reinforced my earlier decision during that moment of clarity to quit drinking.

After a few months, Mike saw that I was serious about my recovery, and we became closer than ever before. Once we compared our medication that the shrinks had us on. When I told him I was taking ten milligrams of this medication, he said he was prescribed only five milligrams. I mentioned the next drug I was taking at twenty milligrams, he said he was prescribed only ten milligrams. We laughed as we decided that I must be twice as screwed up as he was. He and I stayed sober for several years before he quit going to AA meetings and became withdrawn. His addiction was back and apparently in full force. He ended up out of a job, divorced, and living in a friend's small rental home when he called his ex-wife on the phone, put a gun to his head, and shot himself with her on the other line. I'll never forget receiving the call telling me that he had been transferred to Grady Hospital in Atlanta. It was devastating.

Another old friend called to tell me Mike had shot himself and offered to drive down to Atlanta together. I remember crying as I waited on my buddy to pick me up. We arrived at Grady Hospital a little over an hour later. The conversation as we drove down was one of shock and anger. It pissed us off that Mike was so selfish.

If you've never been to Grady Hospital, then please don't go unless you absolutely have to. I'm not saying it's in a bad neighborhood, but it's the only hospital I've ever seen that had metal detectors in the emergency room. The place is rough. What amazed me as we entered the intensive care waiting area was that even though this place was an hour and a world away from Winder, there were already people from Winder starting to gather in support of Mike and Tammy. By the time the doctors came out and told us that he was brain dead and that we needed to make a decision as to keep him on life support or not, more than twenty friends had gathered in the hospital. We were given a chance to visit his lifeless body before Tammy had to make the decision. Mike died that afternoon.

To this very day, it pisses me off that he had so many people who loved and supported him, and yet he felt so lonely and unloved as to take his own life. That's the thing about suicide, usually someone wants to have the last word in an argument, and by killing themselves they not only get the last word, but they purposely attempt to put the shame on someone else. Walter did it when he killed himself in Mama's house, my cousin did it when she took those pills and hooked a muffler to her window, and now Mike had the last word. He purposely called Tammy to make sure she was on the phone when he pulled the trigger. I don't know how you would describe these acts, but I think it's sick, and I know the person committing suicide is ill. No well person would take his or her own life.

CHAPTER NINE – LAST MAN STANDING

I've always taken great pride in the fact that my son never had to work a day in his youth. I'm also kind of happy that while I was an absentee dad because of divorcing when he was three, that he ALWAYS knew I was there for him and that I had his back. After the divorce, I saw another psychiatrist to help with the anger, sadness, hurt, and confusion that caused me to suffer. He helped me get to a point where I could accept my son's mother's decision, and deal with her in a way that focused on his best interests. From that point on, she and I only discussed my son. If any conversation with her strayed from the topic of him, I didn't participate.

One thing the shrink didn't warn me about was that I might put too much emotional dependence on my son. That's too bad because that's exactly what happened. I put him at the forefront of everything I did.

Our relationship was the backbone of my mental and emotional stability. I can't say that I was stable during those years, but without him in my life, I'm pretty confident that I'd have ended up losing complete touch with reality and falling into the pit that my other brothers had fallen. I did everything that I could for that boy, both in time and in money, and to my knowledge, I never beat him, cussed him out, or made him work a day in his youth. That was the only way I could show my love, and it's a hell of a lot better than the way I was raised.

I was the 'Grade Mother' for his first six years of school. Every holiday or special school event, I could always find in my mailbox a letter reading "Dear Grade Mother," and I'd get all pissed off about their sexist attitude. His mom was very generous in allowing me to pick him up from school and to meet him at his bus stop. She made sure he knew I was there. Hell, I even coached a few years of soccer. I took the boy on umpteen cruises, to World Series ballgames. We visited Alaska, Hawaii, Mexico, and Italy. I thought he knew I was there for him.

What I really take pride in is that he's grown up to be a good man. After completing college, he joined the ministry and became an on-campus chaplain at Georgia Tech. He's now back in medical school, married to a teacher he met when doing his ministries. His wife comes from a large and loving family, and they've taken him in as one of their own. They say that when the daughter marries you gain a son, but that when your son marries you lose a son. That just seems to be the nature of things, and he's definitely migrated toward his wife's family. For some reason I never saw that coming, I thought we'd always hang out and that he and I would stay close and well connected. I'm glad that he's found a great caregiver in his new wife, and that he's in a family whose definition of normal is far removed from mine. He and his wife are raising my grandsons in a loving, stable, and Christian home. How cool is that?

It's strange how I feel when I'm around them now. I get the definite impression that my personality doesn't sit well with them. Both my son and I are head strong and stubborn, and it seems we've come to an impasse in how we now see the world or at least in how we see me being involved in his new family's life. He's made it clear to me on more than one occasion of how he's going to raise a better Langford. My response is that he doesn't have much competition, but when I think about what he's saying, I really want to support his efforts.

We met for breakfast recently and spent the time talking about how he'd come to terms with me being a little crazy, but that he was concerned about exposing his kids and his family to my erratic behavior. Apparently, my use of profanity and offhand comments had taken their toll. He tried to convince me that I wasn't being left out of the kid's lives, but when I consider how little I see them and how many times my requests have been rebuked, it's obvious to me that he feels I'm a negative influence in his family's life, and he's trying to reduce my influence with them. It broke my heart when he told me I wasn't invited to his upcoming thirtieth birthday party. Looking back, I couldn't say, "After all I've done for you." But instead, I realized I could honestly say, "After all I never protected you from, I agree with you." I hadn't done what he needed most, which was keeping him away from the insanity of my family. I didn't protect him from the insanity of them Langford boys. I didn't protect him from seeing me go through three wives and all the emotional turmoil that goes with that. Most of all, I didn't hide our addictive personalities and manic depression from him. The truth is, I did the best I could. I had no idea that my normal was fucking up his normal.

It's important that I mention something here, and it has to do with this book and the 'insane' mission I'm on to share my story. I made a huge mistake in the way I went about writing and presenting this book to my son. While I had given him a copy to read, he never read it, and I never insisted that he do so. When he did read it, he wasn't pleased, and I don't blame him. He told me that he views the book as an ego trip for me and as a way for me to play the role of victim. He believes my telling of the things I've witnessed as airing the sins of others so that my sins are lessened. Hell, I don't know, he may very well be right. I know very well that I have the ability to fool myself and run on self-righteousness to the point of coming off as a bully. The question in all of this for me is what is actually driving me to work this hard to remind myself of all this insanity. Is it for my ego, or is it a higher power driving me?

I've asked myself, my mentors, my friends, and anyone with whom I've shared this project to tell me what they think my motives are. Almost everyone viewed my effort as a brave and powerful one that might help others.

I've worked my entire life to overcome the circumstances of my genetics and the way I was raised, and he's benefitted from my efforts. He has come to reject the idea that my genetic history has any value. It's up to me to bring this story to a place of redemption. The only way I know how I can do that is to make my story public so that others can know they are not alone, they have options, and they can avoid these killers. If using my experiences can redeem others then surely my son can redeem me. On a generational level, I'm tired of my bloodline being stalked. If I can put light on the stalkers, they can't hide in the shadows.

Now let me tell you how I came to sit down and write all of this. I'm on another mission from GOD, and here's how it goes.

GOD's Next Plan for Me

I mentioned earlier the experience that I had in that church in Chile, that overpowering sense that I needed to travel to California to visit my friend Keith. I haven't mentioned the overall effect of that trip and how it returned me to my first true passion in life, which is my passion for making people laugh. The message that GOD sent me in Chile was not for the intent of my saving Keith's life, but for me to be introduced into a way to use my GOD-given talents, my GOD-given suffering, and my family's history in a way that might be of service to others who have suffered or who are suffering from the same insanity that I've experienced. So let me tell you how it came to be that you're reading these ramblings right now.

First of all, let me tell you how I ended up in Santiago, Chile. You see, I returned to the mortgage business around 2002 and had gotten my game back. I was running hard and making money again. I'd also gotten remarried to a lady who brought me out of my depression. Meeting her snapped me out of being a recluse, and providing for her gave me a new purpose. Unfortunately, both the marriage and the world of banking went to hell in 2008. I got divorced, started a new business, and ended up broke and bankrupt. The only saving grace was that the bankruptcy court allowed me to keep my business and the real estate it was on. I was as devastated financially as I had ever been.

Then I got lucky. My business took off, the tractor manufacturer Caterpillar purchased and built a huge plant across the street from the business, my real estate value doubled, and I met a beautiful Cuban Ph.D. at a Georgia-Florida football game. I was back, but not for long.

While my relationship with Dr. Amalia Alvarez was going great, my relationship with my business partner had gone to hell in a hand basket. We agreed to split, he bought my share of the business, and we retained the real estate together. I was flush with cash, no job, and Amalia suggested we visit Santiago. Amalia literally travels the world, and when I came out of the church and told her I was going to California, she didn't flinch, she just asked when I was going.

About a week before my flight out to visit Keith, I ran into a friend from my youth and mentioned I was headed to Los Angeles to visit Keith. The buddy mentioned that his son had gotten a degree in the arts and was living in L.A. I reached out to his son and met up with him once I landed in L.A. During our visit he said he had to run to Flapper's Comedy Club in Burbank for a comedy audition. I asked if I could join him, and he agreed. From there the story gets strange. I won't bore you with the details, but I was allowed to audition, and I was called back from the audition. I extended my stay in L.A. and was placed in a comedy contest at the club. I won the contest, and I was given a chance to perform in a live show where I received a lot more laughs than the headliner.

To be fair, I should tell you that just before my daddy died back in 1996, I had started doing a little standup comedy and had gotten a couple of spots at the famous Punch Line Comedy Club in Atlanta. I had maybe two months of practice when we got the news that Daddy had cancer. With all the trauma of the funerals to follow,

I never had a chance or an ambition to return to comedy. I had postponed going back on stage because I just hadn't felt like being funny, and I had other matters to attend to.

Since I had extended my stay, I figured I might as well see and do as much of L.A. as I could. I took a couple of improv classes, went to a few shows, and spent a lot of time with my young friend from Winder. Over the course of the next two weeks, I had a great chance to see how the comedy business and entertainment business works in L.A., and I didn't see any way to make a living unless it was low budget. While watching this little production of a one man show, it hit as to how I could deliver my message. I'll do a one man show telling the story of dysfunction that I've been sharing with you.

When I returned to Athens, I started writing this book. Once I got a good start on it, I realized that I didn't have the skill set to tell this story to an audience so I sold my home in Athens, found a job back in the mortgage business, and moved much closer to Atlanta in order to gain the skills necessary to be comfortable in my presentation. I started taking improv classes and doing standup comedy again. If you thought the previous pages where unusual, then by all means continue reading, because it gets strange from here.

When I decided that I'd come back into the mortgage world, I had one major requirement. Whomever I worked with had to already know me and have some idea of my strange ways. I was lucky that most of my earlier associates had now become owners of their own companies, so I was able to interview them versus them interviewing me. They all knew I was a top producer, they all knew I was fun to be around, and they all knew that I had faced my battles. I chose the one that showed me the most love, and I started working in Atlanta. I would stay late on nights where I knew there would be an open mic at a local comedy club, and then I'd drive to the club to beg to get three to five minutes performing. It was terrible. I'd get to the clubs early, sign the list and wait around for hours only to find out I didn't get up, or that I'd only get three minutes, but I kept going. My biggest hope was that another comedian would like what I did and help me figure out how to grow my talents. I got that break at the Punch Line Comedy Club almost sixteen years to the day from when I had performed on that very stage before my family's death march began. It was December and a cold and rainy evening as I drove toward the club.

As usual I had gotten to the club early and signed the list. There was a pretty good crowd, and the manager assured me that he'd give me five minutes to perform. I was stoked, and ready to do the usual routine that I had been practicing for a couple of months. The club has a small room off to the side where the comic performing gathers just before going out onto the stage. It's what they call a green room, but it's painted black, and smells like cat piss. There's a small monitor so that you can see the performance, and there is writing on all the walls. It's a cramped little place with about five comics and the host crowded together. I was told that there was one guy in front of me, and then I would perform immediately after him. It was ten thirty at night, I was exhausted from my workday, and I just wanted to go up and go home.

Just before the guy in front of me was to go up, the host tells us we are being pushed back in the order. That's not unusual, but he told us it was because Chris Tucker had shown up and was going to perform. If you don't know that name you should. Chris is a major movie star, and a hugely popular black comedian. My first thought was that this could be my chance to be seen by someone who would see my talent. During the middle of Chris doing his set, the host comes in again and tells us that we are being pushed back again because Marcus Combs is here. My first thought is "who the hell is Marcus Combs," but the other comics in the green room are fired up to hear his name. I couldn't believe that I might get seen by two influential comics on the same night.

The guy in front of me finally went up, and I was told that I would only get three minutes and not a second more. My heart was pounding as I changed my plan, waiting to go out to perform. I decided to junk all of the canned material I had been practicing and just go out there and be Greg. As much of my personality that I could gather I would give to the audience. I don't even remember the routine I did, but I do remember coming off the stage to high fives, and congratulations from the manager of the club. As I looked around the club, I noticed that both Chris and the other guy had already left. Apparently, neither of them saw my show, or if they did, they weren't impressed.

I left the club tired and a little disappointed, but just as I was getting into my car, I saw the host of the show smoking a cigarette out back and talking to this guy. I figured I should thank the host for giving me time, so I walked up to him and this other guy and told him thanks. I didn't even acknowledge the other guy, I just wanted to be polite and head on home. Just as I shook the host's hand, the other guy started telling me that I was funny but that I was "stepping" on my jokes. I'm sure I had a look of confusion on my face when I turned to this bald-headed black guy. I told him I had no idea what he was talking about. He started telling me how I needed to slow down, give the audience a chance to laugh, and then go into the next joke. I asked if he was famous or something, and the host starts laughing, and says, "This is Marcus Combs man, this man is a beast, Def Comedy Jam, Bad Boys of Comedy, he is the shit." I was taken aback as the host threw his cigarette to the ground and ran back in to the club to introduce the next act.

As we stood there, I asked Marcus if he could give me some advice. I told him I was serious about this comedy thing, but didn't have a clue as to how to develop my talent. Marcus told me that he and his other black friends were laughing their ass off at my set, but that the 'white' crowd wasn't getting it. He flat out told me that I needed to be doing 'black' crowds. From my perspective, I didn't care if the crowd was white, black, yellow, or made up of billy goats as long as they laughed at my jokes, and I would get time to develop my skill set. Marcus gave me his number, and I headed home as excited as I can ever remember. I called my buddy Keith, who was still living in California, and told him I had possibly found a mentor.

I tried calling Marcus a few times over the weeks to come. Every once in a while he would get back to me. It seemed he was always out of town performing, he was entertaining the troops in Korea, or on a Steve Harvey Cruise, or in Costa Rica somewhere, but we'd touch base by phone each time he returned. I'll never forget the call I got from him on Saturday the fourteenth of February. It was Valentine's Day, and Amalia was out of town. I was spending the day alone when around two thirty that afternoon the phone rang. It was Marcus, and he told me he had a set for me that night. He was headlining this 'urban' club called Taboo 2, and I was to be there by eight that evening. I was scared and extremely excited at the same time. As soon as I hung up the phone, I immediately started practicing my routine in the mirror and timing it on my watch. This was my chance to shine.

I rehearsed the routine in my head as I drove down to Roswell Road in Atlanta. The GPS told me that the club was a half mile away, but the traffic suddenly came to a halt. As I slowly got closer and closer to the address, I realized the traffic jam was being caused by patrons arriving for the show. Everyone there was black. Not 'urban,' black. I had a lot of black friends growing up in Winder, and the term 'urban' just doesn't apply to them or me. They like to say 'urban' instead of black, but it ain't the same thing. So please don't be offended when I use terms such as black or white. It's just an easy way to describe the situation.

As I turned into the parking lot, I saw a line of couples waiting to get into the club, and they were all dressed up for their Valentine's date. Everyone there was dressed to the hilt, and again, I was the only white guy there. I'm not exaggerating when I say that there were close to five hundred people there. I felt like a speck of salt in a pepper shaker, and in that crowd, I shined like a new penny. As if that wasn't enough, when I walked into the building to find Marcus, I noticed that the stage was set up in the middle of the room. There was no back door, so I would be performing in the round, and if my material wasn't any good, there would be no escape out the back. I was terrified as I gazed inside the club in search of Marcus. When I finally saw him in the VIP section, I almost sprinted to meet with him. He tells the story now of how I came running up to him, talking extremely fast in a high voice, and saying "Marcus, what the fuck have you got me into, I ain't never played more than fifty people at a time, and never a black audience." He just smiled at me, looked straight at me, and reassured me that I was funny and to just have fun. I took that advice to heart as the show began.

If you've never been the only white guy in a black club, let me tell you that at a minimum you feel a small amount of tension. It's obvious you don't fit in, and it's also obvious that people treat you different. It seemed that every table I passed the patrons gave me a strange look, and getting a bartender's attention is difficult. They almost seem too shocked to acknowledge you as you attempt to order a diet coke. I went outside to smoke a cigarette as the host warmed up the crowd. As I lit up a cigarette, I could hear the crowd roaring with laughter. I was going to perform right after the first act, and my heart was pounding out of my chest because the guy in front of me that was performing was hilarious. How on earth was I supposed to follow that?

The short answer is that when the comic finished, and I was introduced, I killed it. I decided just before walking up to the stage to just have fun. I wasn't ever going to have an experience like this again, so I might as well give it all I had. I came onto that stage with all the energy I could muster, and the crowd immediately welcomed me as they laughed at everything I said. I remember spinning around the room and seeing Marcus up in the VIP section smiling his ass off and pointing me out to his friends. I hadn't let him down, and that was really important to me. When I got off stage, I wasn't prepared for the way the crowd treated me that night. Husbands came to me asking to get photos with their wives, single ladies wanted pictures and asked me to dance. I finally felt like I fit in.

My next challenge was to play Uptown Comedy Corner in downtown Atlanta. I would say it was an urban club, but again, it's a black club. It's not only a black club, it's also in a bad neighborhood next to a strip club. Let's just say that I was a long way from Winder. The crowds at Uptown were known to be harsh if you weren't funny, so I went there with a lot of momentum from performing at Taboo 2, and a lot of attitude that I wasn't going to fail. I killed it again, and suddenly I was in the black comedy business. I was on my way to be what I now call myself. I'm Atlanta's hottest Black Comedian. If I only play black crowds then that makes me a black comedian, right? That's my argument, and I'm sticking to it.

In the past ten months since Marcus got me that first gig on February 14, I've played every black club in the Atlanta area, I've filmed a comedy DVD, I've played black clubs Harlem, Queens, and Times Square. I'm headed to Chicago to get in a few sets over the Thanksgiving holiday next week. That's all great, but what I've really gained is a good friend in Marcus and a direction to take my message against the killers. I'm close to being prepared to putting my tragedies to benefit, redeeming myself with my son, and fulfilling GOD's mission that he gave me in Chile only two years earlier.

POSTSCRIPT

A lot of people have told me over the years that I should write a book, and there you have it. To be honest, it reminds me of the first date I had in high school with a girl who was hot and horney. I finally had it and didn't know what to do with it.

I did get most of it down on paper, and to tell you the truth, I don't feel much better. I was fifty-five when I started writing, and I just turned fifty-seven. The first year of writing this stuff down and bringing up these memories was a bitch. I knocked out the body of the book in about a month or so, but had to step away and revisit the story several times. It just hurt too much to be this honest. Who am I kidding? This ain't no story, it's my normal, and it hurts to see it in writing. I became depressed, agitated, and withdrawn from the world for more than just a few weeks. More than one friend called to check on me, my co-workers thought that my face seemed flushed and that I might have a stroke.

To top it off, during the time of my writing, Robin Williams committed suicide. It's surreal that while I'm sitting here contemplating bringing awareness to addiction in the form of comedy, my greatest comedic hero kills himself. Don't tell me GOD doesn't like to mess with my head.

I can also tell you that not one of my closest loved ones have died from anything other than natural causes since I started writing this story. It seems strange to take gratitude in the fact that no one has overdosed or killed themselves, but that's normal for me.

When I first sat down to put my story on paper, I had no idea what would come from it. I really thought I'd write a couple of pages and call it a day. What was surprising to me besides the number of pages is that I actually feel that it's helped me come up with a roadmap of how I survived. It wasn't a plan while I was living the insanity, but looking back there are definitely certain actions I took that has saved my life thus far.

If you make any comparisons of my story to your own, please don't. To me, mine was normal, and I hope that you can find your normal and accept it as well. In order for you to do that I hope you've taken away a few pointers of how I've survived. If not, then please allow me to share them again with you here. I'm not saying that my approach is the only one to take, but I truly believe in order to survive the insanity of addiction and mental illness you must remember to consider the following:

1. You have to confront the truth and the situation with all the harshness you can muster. If addiction brings a knife, you must bring a gun. Confrontation is the first and constant step you must take. It may hurt the user, but it might kill the disease. Please go back and read the chapter, "Suicide Survivors" again to see where I underscore this point.

2. Cycles can be broken. We don't have to be what we were born into. We control our own destiny and the destiny of future generations.

3. No one had the ideal families we see on TV that are portrayed as normal. Everyone has his or her own normal, and that's okay. Whatever your dysfunctional family life was like, that is what is normal for you. Recognize it for what it is and use that dysfunction to your advantage.

4. If you don't allow the addict to hit bottom, then you're supporting their addiction and making things worse. They must hit bottom if they are ever going to have that moment of clarity. It's a formula that worked for both my surviving brother and me.

5. Just like time, humor heals all wounds. If you can share a smile during your challenges, you can overcome them. Humor helps you become a survivor rather than a victim.

My wish for you is that you've gained some insight into how to overcome your challenges, and I hope that my story helps you overcome the insanity that comes along with addiction and mental illness. I also hope you find a way to tell your story to others and use whatever your challenges in life are to help others recognize these killers and lessen their destruction. Who knows, maybe one day you will wind up on stage doing a comedy routine around your life tragedies as well. If it gets the message out and lessens the suffering of others, it doesn't matter what the delivery system is, as long as the message gets out.

THANK YOU

Thank you for reading *Heroically Well Adjusted*. I hope you enjoyed the story of my life, taking from it whatever you can to help you through the dysfunction of your life or the lives of those around you. If you liked my story, I'd appreciate it if you wrote a short review on the retail site where you purchased the book. It would go a long way in helping me get my message out to others and help me in fighting these killers the only way I can.

Contact Information:
Facebook: http://on.fb.me/1ODM6dL
Email: glangford60@yahoo.com

ACKNOWLEGEMENTS

As I've read other books, I've noticed that it's customary to place the acknowledgements at the front of the book, but like a lot of things, I'm going to do it backwards and place it at the end. I think it more fitting. So let me thank the people without whose involvement in my life, this story would have never had to be written. The first acknowledgments are to all those people who shaped my youth. The second group are the friends and loved ones who helped me overcome the first group's influence.

To those who influenced my youth

First of all, let me thank both my mother's and my father's ancestries. No family gets this fucked up in one generation, and neither did this one.

I'd also like to thank the community of Winder and Barrow County, Georgia. Without your culture of drinking, drugging, and raising hell, I don't think I would be writing this. You always raised the bar in being a dumb ass, and the Langford boys were always up to that challenge.

To all the high school kids over sixteen years of age back in the 1960s and early '70s who drove through the Triangle and gave me hell. If you hadn't tested me so often, and at such a young age, I don't think I'd have reached my potential as a smart ass. Humor works better than killing myself.

To those who helped me overcome my youth

To Mike, the first guy who ever took me to an AA meeting. He was one of my best friends since high school. Mike's death has always been a mystery to me in that when the word went out to his friends, he literally had almost twenty people drive over an hour to the worst part of Atlanta, go through a metal detector, and sit in the emergency room just to support him and his wife, Tammy. It still blows me away how many people loved him. All my experiences have been without any support and with no one there. I loved you, Mike, and so did everybody who knew you.

To Tammy, Mike's widow. Tammy convinced me to go seek help and go to rehab. If not for her intervention, I have no doubt that I would have died a slow and useless death.

To Aamir, my best friend in the banking world and my professional career. Decades ago, I was lucky enough to have hired you once, but you've returned that favor several fold over the years. Your friendship and our times together have been a haven for me when the world started really kicking my ass. I always appreciated the fact that we could talk about anything, and I never felt judged, plus you made a great wing man. Thanks for taking all those calls over the years when I'd reach out to you for advice and guidance. We both know I rarely took your advice, but I really appreciate you being there to offer it.

To Keith, my best, longest, and dearest friend who has always been there for me. He and I have been through first grade, Cub Scouts, college, kids, crying, and surviving because of each other. I especially appreciate the time he spent in California. It was great calling him at 1:30 in the morning panicked and knowing it was only 10:30 there. He and his wife Vicki have moved back to Georgia now, and they have been a Godsend for me. His wife Vicki is an angel; she's not only put up with Keith for all these years, she's put up with me. That woman should be recommended for sainthood.

There's another Saint Vicki that I'd like to acknowledge. She's the wife of another great friend of mine, Don. Don and Vicki sheltered me during some rough storms and saw me at my unbridled worst. It's always been a great comfort that whatever else might fail me, I have a haven. I've told them before that my backup plan was to move into their attic above their garage. It's comforting to know that they were okay with that.

To all three ex-wives, I apologize for taking you hostage, but I paid a heavy ransom. It's not like I ever hid who I was or how I was raised. At some point, we all thought we were in love. Love is blind and marriage is eye surgery. Either way, I hope that when you look back, you don't only focus on the hurts. If you focus hard enough, I'm sure you can find a couple of times where we laughed our asses off. I know you've given me enough material to laugh my ass off. Try to stick to those.

I especially want to acknowledge my son's mother. She and I were high school sweethearts, and she saw the family in all of its glory. Yet she stayed with me for fourteen long years. I have no idea how she lasted ten years married to me. Since the divorce so long ago, she has been there when I really needed support. She's the only person on earth that knew all the players in this drama. It never failed that when I had emotional or mental problems and needed to reach out to someone, she was there. Thank you, Jennifer.

To my son, the cornerstone of my focus and my reason for living for way too many years. I put too much emotional dependence on you at an early age. I'm sorry, son, for handing you these genes, but at least you know about them. You've been a better man than I have for too many years now, and I am making every effort to step up my game. If I can just get you to be a tenth as proud of me as I am of you, I'll die a happy man.

To my two grandsons, the next generation of Langford boys. I'm not sure if you'll get the chance to know me any better than I knew my grandfathers. When and if you read all of this, I want you to know how proud I am that your father made the right choices and had the opportunity to be a better man than any Langford boy mentioned. It's your father's choices that have given you a better shot of being a better Langford than any of us. Don't blow it—if you've read this then you know that you've got a pretty good chance of being pre-disposed to the killers I've been talking about. I just want you two to know what insanity looks like in your family so that you'll be aware that the killers are in your genes. It would be great if you someday read this and knew how I've had a small part in giving you a chance to beat the odds of addiction and suicide. You might not get to know me personally, but my efforts to break the cycle are what have given you a chance to have a 'normal' that was much better than previous generations.

A Final Acknowledgement

I don't know if this type of acknowledgement is customary or not, but I've got to give special recognition to Patricia Zick. There's no way this book would have been as detailed or as long if Pat hadn't agreed to be my editor. What I originally sent her was about 30,000 words, and an organized outline of a story. Pat's blunt direction, inquiries, and encouragement are what compelled me to write the story you've just read.

I can't tell you if she adopts every new author the way she adopted me, but I am more than grateful for what she has done to make this book possible. Pat not only edited, proofed, and inspired me to write, she formatted, downloaded, synchronized, and did whatever computer-related stuff that needed to be done to get my book listed on the all the retail sites where the book is now available.

Best case, without Pat, I'd either have an unfinished project or a personal story that I'd only share on occasion. It was Pat's efforts, honest opinion, and experience in journalism that gave me the product and the opportunity to share my story with you.

If you've ever decided to write your own book then I'd like to give you two pieces of advice. One is to start writing now because it takes more time than you think, and the second is to get in touch with Pat if you plan to have a quality finished product. You can email her at pczick23@gmail.com for more information.

APPENDIX – MY STAND UP ROUTINE

How y'all doin'? I'm Greg Langford, from Winder, Georgia. Anybody here ever heard of Winder? I'm surprised; especially considerin' the tourism board is only a two by four.

Being from Winder, people often think I'm a bit backwards, but that ain't so. I happen to have worked for the largest banking companies in Atlanta. Yeah, I'm part of their affirmative action program. I'm their token redneck.

To be honest, until I came to work at Atlanta, I thought a bagel was a hunting dawg.

I also thought Times Square was one of them new math problems

People tell me that I don't act like I'm from Winder, and I tell 'em when I'm in Winder I do. The fact is that I do behave differently when I'm in Winder than when I'm in Atlanta.

For instance, when I'm in Atlanta I wear my Versace, when I'm in Winder I wear camouflage. In Atlanta I raise my hand to hail a cab to pick me up, when I'm in Winder I raise hell in the cab to my pick up.

There's other similarities as well.

Atlanta has panhandlers. We do too, only ours work at the Waffle House.

Y'all have crack whores. We have cousins.

In Atlanta, you can get a sex change. If you want a sex change in Winder, you get a divorce,

I tell you the one I feel sorry for about having a sex change is Chas Bono. She was Sonny and Cher's daughter until she got a sex change and became Cher's son. I saw her the other day on TV, and she's gained 225 pounds. Can you imagine going to all that trouble to get a penis and then not be able to see the damn thing?

There's another famous transgendered person in the news these days, and it confuses me and makes me question everything I've known since 1976. That's Bruce Jenner. Bruce was a hero back in the day, and we all idolized him for his success in the Olympics. His picture was on a box of Wheaties, which was a big deal back in the day. Can someone please tell me how you go from Wheaties to Titties? I mean, all this time I was looking up to him, he could have been going down on me. This guy went from being a bad ass to being a bad piece of ass.

I've been divorced three times, and I blame it on advice I got from my daddy. He always told me to notice how a woman acts on a first date because that's the way she'll treat you in six months. Sure enough my first date with my first wife, she never looked at the waiter, she just looked at me and said, "Tell him I want a steak, tell him I want it rare, and tell him I want a side salad." Ten years later, she and I are sitting at the attorney's office, and she won't look at me, but looking straight at the attorney she says, "Tell him I want the house, tell him I want child support, and tell him I want alimony."

My first date with my second wife went great. She was friendly to the waiter, joked with him, and when I came back from the bathroom, she was giving him a blow job. I had to marry THAT woman.

I knew it was over with my first wife because she let work come between us. That's right, she married her boss. My second wife gained 138 pounds the first year we were married. I had always wanted to sleep with two women at the same time, I just never thought that she'd be both of 'em. To be fair, she had a hearing problem. She thought the preacher said "in THICKNESS and in health"

I'm not saying that my third wife and I didn't get along, but I once bought her a half dozen roses and she gave me six "fuck you's."

I've paid alimony, child support, and lump sum payments. If you think Obama Care is expensive, you should try 'Old Mama Care.'

I happened to go out to Los Angeles last year for a couple of weeks and found out I've been living the L.A. Lifestyle all along. I mean, I've not only been married three times, I've gone to rehab.

It's true, I haven't had a drink since February 3, 1999. I haven't smoked a joint in twenty minutes.

And I've really been to rehab. Has anyone else here been to rehab? Okay. some of y'all are lying, but I guess it's just me and Lindsay Lohan. I used to say Amy Winehouse, but that didn't work out so well.

You know Amy died at twenty-seven, just like Jimmy Hendrix, Janis Joplin, and Kurt Cobain. They were all part of that curse of twenty-seven where celebrities die at twenty-seven years of age. Y'all know what that means? It means we only have six more years to put up with Justin Bieber.

There's really something to this curse of twenty-seven though. Think about it, Michael Jackson and I were the same age. He died when he was fifty-four. He had twenty-seven years as a black guy, and twenty-seven years as a white guy.

I've got to admit, I wasn't excited about going to rehab. But I knew I had a problem when I went through the drive-thru at McDonalds and ordered just a straw. The kid asked me if I wanted fries with that. I told him, "No, I'm getting fried with that."

Hell, just yesterday in the bathroom I thought I was having a drug flashback, turned out to be just a piss shiver.

I once got drunk and took a dog tranquilizer. I woke up two hours later curled up in a corner with a bad taste in my mouth and my balls licked raw. I said to myself, "Ain't that some shit" turned out it was, it was between my teeth.

When I first got to rehab I was a little belligerent, and very argumentative. They told me I was bipolar, I told the doctor that he obviously didn't know me. I am HETERO POLAR.

One shrink came in and told me that I was BP, AADD, and definitely suffered from PTSD. Then he asked me if I had any questions. I said yeah, "Can I buy a vowel?"

I eventually self-diagnosed myself as having southern turrets, all I had to do was quit drinking and keep my mouth shut.

Rehab was actually a great place to be. The food was great, the people were interesting, and you got to play volleyball once a day. When I was there it was a twenty-eight day program, and ever the over achiever, I graduated in twenty-seven days. I've still got one day left.

You actually meet a great and varied bunch of people in rehab.

I met doctors, shrinks, sex addicts, eating disorder victims, and Alzheimer's patients.

There were five dentists there. It seems that in addition to Trident Sugarless Gum, four out of five dentists recommend nitrous oxide.

There was a stripper there, and she had a crack problem. She checked out early because her song came up.

The toughest people to release are the sex addicts. That's because every time you tell them that they're getting discharged, they have a relapse.

I met this very famous country singer that was there suffering from Alzheimer's. He was working on a new song titled "I would forget you baby, but I already have."

They kicked me out of a suicide survivors meeting because I kept insulting their marksmanship and knot-tying abilities.

I dated an anorexic girl, but that didn't work, she wouldn't swallow. .

You may think that that's an anorexic joke but it ain't. It's a bulimic joke, because I shoved it down your throat, and you threw it back up on me.

After we broke up, I dated a schizophrenic girl, but that didn't work out either because I couldn't get used to dating two women at the same time

I'm still addicted to cigarettes. I actually feel sorry for the non-smokers because they're missing out on the benefits of smoking. There are some great benefits to smoking that you might not have considered. I smoke for three reasons, health, economics, and quality of life. My fiancé told me she read a survey in *Cosmo* and sixty-five percent of women wouldn't date a smoker, I told her that ninety-five percent of the women wouldn't date me so smokin' improved my odds.

They say kissing a smoker is like kissing an ashtray. That just ain't true. I know because I got lonely one night and tried. I cut my tongue in two places. It was hot though, I guess I should have put the cigarette out first.

There are some great health benefits to smoking as well. I went to the doctor, and he told me I needed to lose weight and that my cholesterol was high. He then said I needed do some aerobics. I asked him what that would do, and he said it would raise my heart rate, help me lose weight, and put a little stress on my lungs. I said hell; I'll just smoke another cigarette. I figure each cigarette I smoke is worth a quarter mile. I'm smokin' five miles a day. On the weekends, I can smoke a marathon.

Think about it, that's why marathon runners and cancer patients have the same body type. Watching some of these races, you don't know if the guys running towards the finish line or running from an iron lung.

The second reason I smoke is economics. You figure that in Georgia a pack of cigarettes cost five dollars. That means every cigarette costs twenty five cents. Watchin' these anti-smoking ads, they say that each cigarette has roughly one thousand chemicals. Hell, I'm getting forty chemicals for a penny. You tell me a better deal in this economy, and I'll kiss your ass. I can't afford not to smoke.

The third reason I smoke is a quality of life issue. They say every cigarette you smoke takes away three minutes from your life. I don't know if I mentioned it or not, but I've been married and divorced three times. I did the math, and if I smoke eight hundred eighty six thousand two hundred and twelve cigarettes, I can completely wipe those three women out of my life.

I'm getting old now. When I was younger I used to cut my bangs when they touched my eye brows, now I cut my eyebrows when they touch my bangs.

When you get older, hair starts growing from everywhere it wasn't and falling out from everywhere it was. When I went for my last haircut, the barber asked me if I wanted to start with the left nostril or right. I showed him. I told him to start with my ears.

I went to one of these hair replacement centers to price out getting hair plugs for my widow's peak. They tried to sell me their top model. It's called a pubic zirconium; I declined when I found out where they took the plug from.

I grew up as the only red head out of five kids. Have you got any idea of how much a red-headed kid gets picked on? I'm not saying that everybody picked on me, but even my dad called me carrot top. I got so pissed off so I paid the kid next door to play my part in the family movies.

I mean it was tough! Besides getting called carrot top and pecker head, when I was seven I almost committed suicide due to all the times I'd been told "I'd rather be dead than red on the head."

When I was eight I shampooed in Visine, because I heard it would get the red out.

It was supposed to be good luck to rub a red-headed kid on the head, so old men would rub my head all the time and ask me, "Where'd you get that red hair." I'd run hand up my face, act like I'd blown my nose in my hand, and rub it across my head and tell I had a nose bleed.

The worse one of all was "red on the head like a dick on a dawg." That was bad enough, but someone later added "Ugly in the face like tits on a hawg."

I figured out my sex life is over forty-three years long. For anyone less than forty-two years, got some good news and some bad news. The bad news is that I could have slept with your mother; the good news is that I did it when she was hot. I've slept with everything from jail bait to miltfs. I'm now dating griltfs, that's grandmothers I'd like to fraternize with.

About ten years ago, I was dating this older woman. I was forty-seven, and she was sixty-nine. She was hot though. I mean, she had been augmented, sucked, plucked, and deserved to be fucked. It turns out she was a great, great grandmother. Y'all know what that made me? A great, great grandmother fucker.

I remember this same woman telling me that she was a cougar. I had to tell her that at her age she was a saber tooth. I told her that I was her boy toy, and she told me that if I were a toy, I'd be a slinky.

I quit dating young girls. A young woman has hot flashes; an old woman has hot meals.

Also, an older woman knows more about sex than a younger woman. This one woman showed me a sex move that a non-young woman can possibly do. You won't find this move in the Kama Sutra, and it ain't written on no walls or bathroom stalls. It's called a 138. Got any guess what that is? It's when you have sixty-nine with a sixty-nine –year-old woman.

You women might not know this, but older men use age averaging when we date. For instance, if a guy who's thirty dates a twenty-year-old, he takes the average as him being twenty-five. A forty-year-old dates a twenty-year-old so he can be thirty. Hell I figured it out the other day, for me to be in my thirties, I'd have to date an embryo. It probably won't happen, but I've been fantasizing about a three-way with a zygote.

Y'all don't have to worry about me anymore, at my age it's not that I've lost my sex drive, it's that I don't even want to crank the car.

I'm not a threat to women anymore because my testosterone has shrunk, and my prostate has enlarged.

I've really been married and divorced three times. You've heard of being a serial monogamous, I'm a serial monotonous. I've lived by the motto of the only thing worse than being alone is wishing you were.

If I marry another woman who's been married three times as well, that will make eight marriages between us. I guess that would make us oxymorons.

You'd think that having been married three times would be an advantage to dating women, I hear women all the time complaining about finding a man who can make a commitment. Come on ladies, nobody commits more than me.

I've tried to figure out what went wrong with my marriages, and I'm convinced it ain't me. It ain't them. It's the institution. I mean the concept of modern marriage came around when people's life span was only twenty-five years. Back then everybody got married at thirteen and died at twenty. Romeo and Juliet were only twelve and thirteen. The only reason people back then stayed married for life is that they died after seven years. That's why we now get the seven-year itch.

That's why I've come up with a totally new marriage product. I've merged my four decades of banking with twenty five years of married life and come up with the solution. When you get a mortgage, you're offered either a fixed rate, called an ARM, or an

Adjustable Rate Mortgage. I've come up with an Adjustable Rate Marriage. ARM.

That's right ladies and gentlemen, instead of being put into a permanent rate marriage product, I can put you into an ARM. Just like mortgages, these products would come in three, five-, seven-, or ten-year terms.

I would suggest the seven-year ARM. Imagine how relationships would change if you knew you were contractually obligated to end or renew the deal? As it got closer to renewal time, men would start losing weight, doing the laundry, and finally putting the seat down. And women would stop coming to bed in those damn woolen night gowns. I bought my second wife woolen sheets just so she could come to be naked.

ABOUT THE AUTHOR

Most often referred to as a "short, cocky, red-headed, smart ass," Greg Langford is a unique individual. His confidence, sense of humor, confrontational manner, and his work ethic are the tools he uses to tell his story of surviving in a home filled with the insanity of addiction, mental illness, and suicide.

Receiving accolades in sports, scouting, academics, community service, business, and comedy, Greg must be considered an overachiever. His story is one that will resonate with anyone who suffered from growing up or still living with the insanity of a dysfunctional family.

Made in the USA
Lexington, KY
20 June 2016